"Brava! Finally, a book that tells the truth about spiritual development. *Noble Soul* is a unique guide to reclaiming essential aspects of a woman's life, truly an 'owner's manual' for the soul. According to this clearly written, non-denominational, and poignant book, life is not meant to be a joy ride. Instead, it is more like a workshop with the potential to transform us. Whether a seasoned student of spirituality or a student of life, this book will teach you how to 'mine your inner gems' and live more fully."

—**MARGO MAINE**, PhD, FAED, CEDS clinical psychologist,
author of *Body Wars: Making Peace with Women's Bodies*
and co-founder of Maine & Weinstein Specialty Group

"*Noble Soul* is one of the most beautiful books on the theme of human empowerment that I have ever read. But more than being beautifully constructed, it also embodies the charm of an engaging autobiography, as well as the ethereal form of a sacred meditation. In this way, it invites the reader into a state of contemplation that few texts of this kind are capable of.

Kadzo has written something more than a 'self-help' book. She has penned, in exquisite prose, a guide for the wayfarer. Women–and men–of every culture and way of life will find in this work a ray of light."

—**MICHAEL PENN**, PhD clinical psychologist, professor of psychology
& coauthor of *Overcoming Violence against Women and Girls:
The International Campaign to Eradicate a Worldwide Problem*

"Kadzo Kangwana takes us on the most critical journey of our lifetime and helps us understand the process of becoming. She shares her life story–from an externally referenced identity from her culture and greater society, to a beautiful discovery of her true self, her spiritual reality–and allows the reader to peer into that reality. *Noble Soul* is a very important read for all women and for anyone who has a female in their life. It helps us understand what empowers human beings and how the feminine needs to walk its own spiritual path to establish its equality."

—JULIE BURNS WALKER, motivational speaker,
author & developer of *The Oneness Model*

"*Noble Soul* is a must-read for any woman seeking wholeness and well-being. It spoke to me as a woman, mother, human, and more importantly as a soul! It awakened me. This book will support women of all backgrounds to understand the importance of the spiritual aspects of their lives. Kadzo guides us on an invaluable journey of inner growth that challenges our understanding of who we truly are, and highlights the critical connection between our mental health and spirituality."

—EMILY BALDONI, actress, entrepreneur
& co-founder of @weareamma

"Our scientific understanding now appreciates that a purely material approach to the body is insufficient and inaccurate. Kadzo Kangwana's book demonstrates the value of recognizing the interplay between psychology and spirituality. Acknowledging the existence of a deeper reality and choosing to see ourselves and relate to others from this vantage point profoundly affects our day-to-day experience and sense of well-being. The degree to which we mine our spiritual capacity impacts how we weather physical, mental health, relational, and other challenges. *Noble Soul* is the book we need in this moment: an offering that affirms and addresses the heart of what ails us."

—FARANEH CARNEGIE-HARGREAVES,
DC founder of @drfaraneh and @bejoyseekjoy

"Kadzo effectively moves among her own life experiences, spirituality, clinical experience, and theory to produce a book that can help women effectively maneuver through the complexities of current society. It not only teaches but provides a handbook of specific steps that women can take to enhance confidence, self-esteem, and self-understanding. It fills a large gap for so many women who struggle to find contentment in this world. *Noble Soul* was wonderful and inspiring to read!"

"This book is an incredible gift. With wisdom, kindness and deep insight, Kadzo gently accompanies us on a joint journey to uncover the connections between our experiences and expressions of spirituality, and our mental health. This generous book is full of hope and optimism, and it is both timely and timeless. It is a guide of and for our time. It is a book for us all."

"*Noble Soul* offers a theoretically sound and universally applicable take on spiritual growth. Kadzo Kangwana makes the seemingly abstract notion of spiritual development both practical and accessible."

NOBLE SOUL

NOBLE SOUL

A GUIDE *to* SPIRITUAL GROWTH *for Women*

KADZO KANGWANA MA, LCSW

Blue Lapis Books
BLUELAPISBOOKS.COM

Printed in the United States of America

Blue Lapis Books | bluelapisbooks.com

LCCN: 2022908105
ISBN: 979-8-9861250-0-8

To Nyanya Mwanasiti
and all the women in my lineage.
Each day I reap the benefits of
your love, vision and sacrifice.

Contents

Recollections: African Girl

The image on the black-and-white photo is still crystal clear in my mind. My mother is wearing a white dress, smiling and holding a newborn baby and I, beside her, look up at them both. It is unlikely, given that I was only two when my brother was born, that I have an actual memory of that moment. Instead, I have many memories of looking at the photo, and hearing my mother say how proud she was to have a son. From an early age, I knew that the baby my mother was holding in the photo was the special one.

I am ten years old and lying on my yellow-and-white bed-spread with most of my school notebooks piled beside me. Each book is neatly covered in brown paper to prolong its life. I am going through them one at a time, looking at my grades and reading my teachers' comments. As I read the positive notes and count the A's, I am both comforted and a little confused. I am looking for evidence of a comment my father just made that I am not as intelligent as my brother. The data does not match my father's observation. Many years later, I see that the comparison was made to encourage my brother.

Time has passed, and I come home from school to see my parents making preparations to travel to our tribal home to

bury my paternal grandfather. Both my mother and father are folding clothes and putting them into small suitcases in between phone calls with family and friends who reach out to give their condolences. My brother is going on the trip with my parents, and my younger sister and I are staying in the city with our nanny. I ask why my brother gets to go and I am told that he is the only son and that he must be there for all the burial rituals.

I am eighteen and it is just weeks before I leave for college. My father takes me on a trip to our tribal home on the Kenyan coast. The air is warm and humid, and we can smell the salty ocean. I greet aunts, uncles and cousins and they welcome me warmly. Surrounded by tall coconut palms, we sit in a circle on tiny three-legged wooden stools that have been pulled out of the thatch-roofed mud homes. I use a stick to draw in the loose brown-gray sand while my elders catch up with each other's news and chickens wander between us. One of my aunts has a chicken slaughtered for us to eat. As we eat sima *and chicken stew, one of my uncles tells me I have brought great honor to the family because I am the first girl from the Giriama tribe to go to Oxford University. He also tells me that I must not forget where I come from.*

I cannot remember the exact moment I consciously understood that in my world being female meant that I was less than. It is likely that the sense of not being enough took hold as a result of many covert and overt communications, all born from centuries-old patterns of thought and behavior which became solidified as culture. Unlike the males in the family, as a girl child I had to earn approval and I had to prove my worth.

Introduction: Welcome!

"Obviously, my thoughts are all over the place," Maxine laughed as she waved her hands in the air with her usual energy. She had been talking animatedly about her job and her romantic relationship, and it was clear to me that she was making steady progress in therapy to address traumatic memories. We had been discussing the ability to observe one's thoughts, and a breakthrough moment came when she looked at me with earnest eyes and said, "So if I'm not my thoughts, who am I?"

This was an elegant landing at the heart of a dilemma that causes mental distress for many of my clients.

"Well, you tell me. Who are you and what is a human being, for that matter?" I asked.

"I don't know. It is hard to say exactly," she responded with a puzzled look.

"So, let's think about it like this: when you say 'my foot,' what is the entity that your foot belongs to?"

"Mmm, I haven't really thought about it like that."

This session with Maxine—and many other similar interactions—has me wondering why so many of us are not clear on who or what we are as human beings. Such existential questions have both challenged us and captivated our imagination throughout history, but it seems that in modern times those struggling with these questions do not always know where to find answers. In the United

States, affiliation to religious institutions—traditionally the source of information on human nature, identity and the meaning of life—has declined in recent years.[1] Paradoxically, this trend reflects a decline in access to information about understanding our nature and potential as human beings, at the same time that scientists are uncovering a profound relationship between our mental health and our sense of ourselves.

As a therapist, I have noticed that one of the consequences of not being grounded in clear information about who we are is feeling an emptiness deep within us. We do our best to fill this void by seeking outside solutions. We look for acknowledgement and validation from others. We focus on our careers, our relationships, our appearance and our social connections thinking that we will feel fulfilled and happy if we just get these things right. The truth is, however, that our efforts to find answers outside ourselves leave us feeling defeated and overwhelmed.

You might be wondering if there is an alternative. Let us imagine for a minute that we are so grounded in our understanding of our true identity that we engage with the world from a place of knowing we are of intrinsic and inestimable value just as we are. This reality is within our reach. The inner peace we are all seeking is directly related to our understanding of who we are at the deepest level of our being. We can think of this deep part of ourselves as the essential self, essence, inner light, inner being, core, spirit, energy or soul. It is the part of us that makes each human unique. In his book *The Power of Now*, Eckhart Tolle refers to this entity as the Inner Being and states that it is the "innermost invisible and indestructible essence."[2] Use whatever language you are comfortable with to name this entity at the very core of who you are. I refer to it as the soul, and all matters related to or concerning the soul as spirituality, but the language used is less important than our awareness and acknowledgement that this part of ourselves exists, and that it is what makes us human.

Like Maxine, when I was in my early twenties I did not have cohesive answers to questions about my core identity as a soul, and looking back on my life's journey I see that I encountered both necessary and unnecessary struggles on the path toward growth. I battled with depression and feelings of inadequacy, while my outward appearance was one of a successful student, career woman and mother. As you will see in the chapters and recollections that follow, without an understanding of myself as a soul and the gifts that each soul brings to humanity, I did not live life on my own terms.

My struggles and the struggles of the women I meet in the course of my work were my motivation for writing this book. My goal is to make the journey of inner growth easier and more efficient, so that we don't waste precious time and can avoid unnecessary emotional pain.

Owner's Manual

This book is about the nature of our inner essence as human beings—our souls—and what we can do to grow spiritually as we navigate the daily concerns of our lives. I have written it because there is a need for an owner's manual on the soul for women of all backgrounds and faith traditions. This is the book I wish I'd had to share with the women who told me they wanted to start a spiritual journey but did not know how to begin, and the women who asked me about ways to enhance or deepen their paths of spiritual growth. I have attempted to focus on themes and use language that speaks to truths that apply to women of all faiths, of no faith and women who are not sure the soul even exists. If there is the faintest whisper in your heart that there might be more to life than our physical reality, this book is for you.

Part One provides perspectives on the connection between spirituality and mental health, and reflections on what it means to be a woman. Part Two presents key concepts for understanding our souls, fostering spiritual growth and navigating the journey of life as women. Between the chapters you will find recollections which are not part of the main text, but reflect themes of spiritual quest and discovery as they rippled through my own life. In sharing these recollections, it is my hope that a piece of my journey might make yours easier, or at least confirm that you are not alone.

The Links between Mental Health and Spirituality

Many of us have been raised without much information about our souls or spirituality, and it is not a coincidence that individuals with no sense of their spirituality experience mental distress. In a study of the adult children of both depressed and non-depressed parents, research scholar on spirituality and psychology, Dr. Lisa Miller and her colleagues found individuals who reported that religion or spirituality was important to them were less likely to experience recurring depression.[3] Using magnetic resonance images of the brain, Dr. Miller and her colleagues also demonstrated that individuals who reported religion or spirituality as being important to them had brain structures that were "thicker and stronger in exactly the same regions that weaken and wither in depressed brains."[4] Examining the relationship between religion, mental health symptoms and substance abuse in a study of female-female pairs of twins, professor of medicine Dr. Kendler and his colleagues found that individuals with high levels of personal devotion showed a less negative response to stressful life events.[5] We also know through research on the neuropsychology of religion, that religious conviction buffers against anxiety.[6]

It appears that the association between our spiritual lives and our mental health and well-being starts early in our lives. Summarizing the results of her research, Dr. Miller writes, "Children who have a positive, active relationship to spirituality" are "40 percent less likely to use and abuse substances" and are "60 percent less likely to be depressed as teenagers."[7]

This accumulating data on the relationship between mental health and spirituality implies that we would do well to attend to our spiritual lives. Referring to the treatment of mental illnesses like schizophrenia and bipolar disorder, professor of psychology Dr. David Lukoff states that for many people, "having a relationship with a higher power is the foundation of their physiological well-being."[8] Author and physician Dr. Jennifer Gaudiani notes in her book *Sick Enough* that recovery from eating disorders requires a client "to remember who she really is and to keep her values at the forefront of her thoughts when she is struggling."[9] The clarity Dr. Gaudiani recommends regarding our identity and awareness of our values falls within the purview of spirituality.

As a psychotherapist, I notice the relationship between mental health and spirituality regularly. At the heart of Maxine's struggle with traumatic memories was the need for her to understand herself at the level of her soul. Of course, when we are speaking of the human soul we are referring to something that defies definition, a reality that cannot be expressed within the confines of human language. It is, perhaps, this difficulty in definitively comprehending the soul that has led us to ignoring it or dismissing its importance. But in being neglectful of our souls, we have only short-changed ourselves. We cannot possibly know everything about the human soul. However, what we do know can provide a foundation for thriving and living a well-grounded life. When we combine the wisdom of the world's spiritual traditions and holy texts with what we can learn from the scientific method, we increase our understanding of our souls and how we can grow spiritually. Dr. David DeSteno, author of *How God Works: The Science Behind the Benefits of Religion*, argues that research indicates science and religion are "two approaches to understanding how to improve people's lives that frequently complemented each other."[10] My own experiences have taught me that science and religion are both valid ways of knowing which, when integrated, can guide us to truth.

Nobility

So what do we know about the soul? The world's great spiritual traditions have taught us that the soul has particular qualities or attributes such as kindness, love, determination and integrity. Our soul's capacity to manifest these spiritual qualities makes us noble beings, and our nobility as human souls is both an invitation to embody our rich spiritual potential and a reminder of our high station as human beings.

We know from scientific research that humans thrive when expressing certain capacities, many of which pertain to the soul. Studying different cultures, professor of psychology Dr. Brett Ford and her colleagues demonstrated that individuals are more successful in their pursuit of happiness when they do so through social connection and generous acts.[11] In research on the neural links between generosity and happiness, psychologist Dr. Soyoung Park and her colleagues demonstrated that individuals who make more generous choices showed stronger increases in self-reported happiness.[12] Both the ability to connect with others and to be generous are capacities of the soul.

A study of 346 military veterans returning to the U.S. from Iraq and Afghanistan showed that volunteering in a civic service program significantly improved their physical and mental health.[13] Service is another capacity of the soul. We are noble souls because each one of us has the potential to manifest the finest human qualities. We all have the capacity to be generous, caring, helpful and just. When we choose to manifest these qualities, we reach toward the highest expression of what it means to be human. A noble soul is our birthright.

Calling All Women

I have chosen to address this book to women because the majority of my clients identify as women and because the soul, although it actually has no gender, has a specific kind of experience when it comes to this planet in a female body. In cisgender women, a distinct biology arises from the brain circuits laid down in utero, as well as the hormonal changes they experience throughout life.[14] This biology, in turn, determines some of the reality of experiencing life as female.

In my work with women, I have observed that many of us struggle with feeling dispensable or disposable. We feel we do not matter, that no one hears us and that what we have to say is of little consequence. Sadly, this has been the feminine experience for centuries in cultures across the globe. However, we now live in an age of great possibility for women. For those of us who experience the despair of being overlooked, those of us who experience the vulnerability of being the unwanted girl child, those of us whose value has been based on the marriages we make, those of us who are paid less for doing the same work as our male counterparts, those of us who struggle with the craziness of hormonal fluctuations and PMS, those of us whose bodies completely transform to grow and nurture new life, those of us who experience the tragedy of being abused because we have a particular set of biological parameters as we emerge from the birth canal, and those of us who made the transition to womanhood later in life, this is our time. Many of the changes we need to improve the lot of women today must occur at the level of governance, policy and attitudinal transformation, but these changes must be accompanied by our own critical inner work and deep effort to nurture our souls and empower ourselves.

As the world continues to awaken to the power of the feminine, and as we take powerful positions across the globe and participate more vocally in all social discourse, we must also be clear on who we are. When we recognize our souls as our true reality and understand how to grow spiritually, we will be happier and more grounded women and all of humanity will thrive.

From Saving Elephants to Empowering Souls

My own path in life has been unusual. My first career was in wildlife conservation. In my early twenties I did doctoral research on elephant behavior and conservation in Amboseli National Park at the foothills of Mount Kilimanjaro. The big blue skies of East Africa are still my happy place, and decades later I can hear the rhythmic sound of elephant trunks reaching for the grass around my tent as I sleep. I also learned how to parent from watching the peaceful and majestic elephant matriarchs interact with their calves, lead their families through terrible droughts and celebrate rainy seasons.

When I completed my studies, I managed wildlife conservation projects across sub-Saharan Africa for a non-governmental organization headquartered in Nairobi. Arriving at work soon after sunrise to play my part in saving wildlife felt fulfilling, but with time I started to question whether the work I was doing was tackling conservation problems at their root. Elephant populations were plunging because people, enticed by the thought of wealth, organized poaching operations, and traders were willing to buy ivory with little thought given to the consequences of their actions. Human motivation and behavior seem to be at the heart of conservation challenges. With these thoughts forming, I left Nairobi for the glorious summers and brutal winters of Ohio and then New Hampshire so my husband could complete his education. Rich memories of days in the field came with me: I had driven Maasai mothers and their sick children to clinics in my small car; I had found solace in the quiet breathing of elephants taking an afternoon nap while I observed their behavior. I remembered my days as a program manager, attending international conferences on biodiversity and meetings with government officials to discuss conservation strategies. As I tended to my two little ones in New

England, I wondered how to create a world where some children did not have to walk miles for water while others, like my own, played with rubber ducks in bubble baths.

Strangely enough, it was in the early days of parenting that the answers to some of my questions began to crystalize. It dawned on me that, as demanding as it was, the time I spent with my children was actually laying the foundation of their characters, the kind of people they might become and the choices they might make in the future. I also began to grasp that if human desires and aspirations lay at the heart of all the planet's crises, then the strategies I employed in my work in conservation needed to be accompanied by a change in human consciousness to be truly successful. This emerging interest in human motivation and behavior led me to embark on a career in mental health in my forties.

Born in Kenya and having lived in England, the United Arab Emirates and the United States, I consider myself a world citizen. I have also been a student of all things spiritual from a young age. Many of my earliest memories are of my nanny, a truly remarkable and kind Muslim woman who, with infinite love and patience, would let me stand next to her and imitate her prayer movements several times a day. I also grew up loving Ramadan, the Muslim month of fasting, because of the special treats my nanny would prepare to break her fast.

My paternal grandfather, an animist who believed that spirits exist in nature, converted to Christianity through the efforts of missionaries working on the Kenyan coast. However, my family held on to some animist practices which meant that whenever I left home on a journey a libation was poured for the ancestors to ensure my safety.

Many years later, in keeping with the animist belief that the spirits are purest in the earliest hours of the day, I was married shortly after midnight in a ceremony that appeased the ancestors with more pouring of libations, as well as much singing and dancing.

All of my school-age years were spent in Catholic schools in Nairobi, and I still know by heart all the right things to say during Mass. When I was twelve, I attended confirmation classes at the Anglican church my family belonged to, and my heart and mind were filled with questions. At the same age, I discovered the work of poet and visual artist Kahlil Gibran and felt like I was drinking from a well of spiritual nourishment as I stayed up night after night reading all his books. Since then, I have investigated multiple faiths and philosophies. In my teens I attended meetings of the Theosophical Society and practiced Rāja Yoga, and while I was at college in England I joined the Christian Union. I was still in college when my world view was shifted dramatically by the truths I found in Helen Schucman's book *A Course in Miracles*, a self-study curriculum on the oneness of God and love. What I have found to be true in my spiritual search is that the essential teachings of the world's spiritual traditions are the same—each of them invites us to a deep and personal relationship with the force that brought us into being, and into more loving and authentic relationships with one another. In my late twenties I found a system of belief in the Bahá'í faith that upholds the essential unity of the world's faiths. I see my spiritual journey continuing for as long as I am on this planet, as I aspire to understand spiritual truths more deeply and live my life accordingly.

I have much gratitude for experiences that have connected me to amazing people across the globe, and I am particularly indebted to my clients whose courage and resilience fills me with awe. Needless to say, I too am striving each day to understand my soul better and grow spiritually, so we are on this journey together. Just as my client Maxine had not yet differentiated between her core identity and her thoughts, when I was twenty I also did not have a clear understanding of my spiritual reality, nor had I claimed my birthright as a noble soul. Ahead, therefore, are ideas which support our spiritual growth as women, as well as notes from the trenches of my own journey toward wholeness. My earnest desire is to give voice to the inner reality of women, and to chart a course for spiritual growth filled with hope and possibility. So, welcome and enjoy!

PART ONE

Perspectives

Recollections:
Seeking Spiritual Truth

It is a sunny day and some of my extended family have gathered at our house. It is the usual affair: adults sitting in circles discussing current events while eating fragrant coconut rice and chicken curry that is spicy enough to make their eyes water, but so delicious they keep eating. I am the guest of honor and I have a new cream dress with a flowing skirt and lace at the waist and hem. The occasion is my confirmation into the Anglican church. That morning I had gone through the church rituals with several boys and girls while our families looked on, but earlier that week I had told my mother that I really did not believe in some of the things I was required to say, and that the priest did not really answer my questions. In response, the pragmatic woman that my mother was negotiated with me, "Kadzo, sweetie. This is one of the things I have to get done for you. First it is baptism and then confirmation. So just say what you have to say on Sunday, then we will have a party and you can wear that nice dress we bought you." I knew better than to argue with her, but I wondered if this was how the world worked. Do I not get to ask questions, and do grown-ups profess their faith without understanding or believing what they are saying?

17

The unpaved road is dry, and soon our shoes are covered in dust from the bright-red volcanic soil of Nairobi. Ben, a well-spoken man in his late twenties, and I are walking to the bus stop after a morning meditation session at the Rāja Yoga Center. The road is flanked with the vivid purple and red flowers of the tumbling bougainvillea bushes, and Ben is telling me how he came to attend the yoga sessions while I listen with interest. He then asks me why a 16-year-old is interested in Rāja Yoga and I tell him I love discussing matters of the spirit, and that I have many questions I am seeking answers to. An old pale-yellow bus pulls up to the stop and Ben takes it. I wait for mine.

There is a knock on my room door in the residence hall and I open it to the president of the Christian Union. She is in her last year of university and I am a little surprised to see her, but I invite her in and offer her a cup of tea. I am thankful I have just tidied my room. She sits on the one chair I have, I sit on my bed and she asks me a number of questions about the weekly Christian Union meetings, my family and how university is going. Some days later there is another knock and another member of the Christian Union comes to visit. We also drink tea and chat about student life.

Toward the end of term, we gather for the usual Tuesday evening supper and Christian Union meeting. I enjoy these sessions because the women who attend are friendly, kind and open to spiritual conversation. I realize even in this gathering I gravitate toward the young women who are open to looking at the deeper meaning of scripture. As supper ends, our attention is called by the president who says she has some announcements to make. She reads the names of the officers for the next year, and I realize the visits to my room were some kind of vetting for positions. I did not make the cut. There is a part of me that knows my mind is open to ways of understanding God and faith that are not welcome in this space, but there is also a part of me that wonders what it means that I am not good enough to serve God in this way.

CHAPTER 1

Soul, Spirituality and Mental Health

"There is only one type of body that's right, and it's skinny. I wanted to be skinny." There was a chilling edge to the way Sonia, a highly intelligent 17-year-old, said these words in response to my questions about the history of her eating disorder. It was her first appointment with me, and I could sense that Sonia did not think she needed treatment. Her mood was sullen, but with a little encouragement to continue, she went on.

"I wasn't happy with the way I looked. Society doesn't like bigger people and I wanted to be liked. Also, when I started losing weight, my friends would compliment me for being so tiny and having no body fat."

I caught my breath with the familiar pain of hearing a young woman disconnected from the core of who she really is. I also felt deep compassion for Sonia while I listened to her describe the impossible standards we have created for women. When I asked Sonia when she thought the concern with her body weight began, she paused for a moment, shrugged her shoulders and said, "Well, in elementary school, people used to tease me and I remember some boys told me I was fat."

At the end of her evaluation, I escorted Sonia back to the waiting room and, in keeping with regular procedure when treating minors, I invited her mother Gilda to come into my office. As Gilda sank into the chair I offered, her eyes teared up and she asked one of the most poignant questions I have heard from a parent.

"How did we get here? How did the things that some kids said in elementary school lead us to this?"

As a therapist specialized in the treatment of trauma and eating disorders, the glimpses I get into the predicament of the feminine are heartbreaking. As women, our bodies are violated in horrific acts of physical and sexual violence. Too many of us have grown up in situations where our basic needs for safety, food and shelter are not met. We are also bombarded with messages that our value is dependent on our physical appearance and the size of our clothes, and we often face this tsunami of chaos, trauma and misinformation without the buffer of having clarity about who we are at our core. Sonia's complete identification with the size of her body is a symptom of a more profound problem. What could have given Sonia an understanding of herself that was broader and deeper than her physical characteristics? What is it that we need to provide for our daughters so they arrive at kindergarten and elementary school immune to the class bullies' teasing? What do we need to resist the onslaught of messages about how much we should weigh or how we should look? As a society, how do we stop the onslaught of emotional and physical violence against women?

Delicate Lock, Wrong Key

Many of the mental health issues we struggle with as women are related to how we think of ourselves. We are not clear about the basis of our identity, what gives us value and our purpose in life. We seek to address the distress we feel about not knowing who we are in the context of mental health treatment often without considering that the foundations of this distress could be spiritual. Questions about identity, value and purpose are actually questions about what makes us human, and are therefore spiritual questions. This connection between spirituality and mental health was observed in the early stages of psychology's development. In his 1933 book *Modern Man in Search of a Soul*, Carl Jung commented that the "psychotherapist must even be able to admit that the ego is ill for the very reason that it is cut off from the whole, and has lost its connection with mankind as well as with the spirit."[1]

We cannot be blamed for not seeing the connection between our mental health and spirituality. Currently, the most widespread and generally accepted mental health treatment techniques are cognitive and behavioral approaches which emphasize changing patterns of thinking and behavior as the main strategy toward building mental wellness. However, our mental health challenges are usually the outcome of a complex interaction between our biology, our history, our beliefs, our patterns of thinking and behavior, and our sense of who we are and what gives us value. While changing our thoughts and behaviors will alleviate some of the symptoms we struggle with, to feel whole and thrive we also need to have a deeper and broader understanding of ourselves.

As a therapist, my goal is to support clients to heal from mental distress and to move toward inner peace and greater effectiveness in their lives. Each client's work generally begins with the goal of reducing symptoms, but as treatment progresses clients often begin to express existential questions that touch on identity and purpose, and a longing to take their place in the world with confidence. This innate desire to thrive is connected to our spirituality, but before we go on to explore the connection between spirituality and our mental health more deeply, let us look at some definitions, so we have a common language for our journey together.

Definitions, Definitions, Definitions

Let us start by clarifying further what we mean by the soul. The world's spiritual traditions, which include the major religions and the spiritual teachings of indigenous peoples, teach us that a human being is made up of both a physical body and a non-physical entity—the soul. These traditions also teach that the soul is what gives life to the physical body. We can think of this as being similar to the way a hand animates a puppet. Michael Singer, author of *The Untethered Soul*, states that the soul is both the center of consciousness from which we can observe and sense the world, and the place from which we are aware of our thoughts and emotions.[2] Let us, then, define the soul as the entity that makes us human and causes us to be aware; the part of us that has the capacity to learn, to understand, to know and to know that it knows. The soul is also the part of us that seeks connection to others and to the source of its being. The power to expand into all that is possible for us comes from our soul.

As we discussed in the Introduction, the human soul has the capacity to manifest spiritual qualities or attributes such as love, kindness, generosity and compassion. What makes us noble souls is the potential to manifest all our attributes and grow into the highest expression of what it means to be human.

A client once asked me if the soul is the product of electrical processes in the brain. There has, indeed, been a system of thinking that attributes our self-awareness to neural connections and chemical reactions. However, recent developments in spiritual psychology are pointing us toward a more expanded understanding of who we are as human beings and moving us closer to accepting what spiritual traditions have always held to be true: there is more to human life than physical existence.[3]

There are nearly as many definitions of spirituality as there are people on the planet. However, a few stand out as being helpful in informing how we can live our lives in ways that support our mental health, and it is those I focus on here. The Merriam-Webster dictionary definition of "spirit" is "an animating and vital principle held to give life to physical organisms,"[4] and "spiritual" is defined as "of, relating to, consisting of or affecting the spirit."[5]

In her book *Soul Talk: The New Spirituality of African American Women*, professor of women's studies and poet, Dr. Akasha Gloria Hull, tells us that spirituality, "involves conscious relationship with the realm of spirit, with the invisibly permeating, ultimately positive, divine, and evolutionary energies that give rise to and sustains all that exists."[6] Dr. Lisa Miller, whose research has provided us with much data on the influence of spirituality on mental health, defines spirituality as follows: "Spirituality is an inner sense of relationship to a higher power that is loving and guiding. The word we give to this higher power might be God, nature, spirit, the universe, the creator, or other words that represent divine presence. But the important point is that spirituality encompasses our relationship and dialogue with this higher presence."[7]

Another definition of spirituality worth noting is from Dr. Eileen Eppig who states that spirituality involves a longing to overcome personal concerns and engage in the process of improving society and building a better world.[8] This definition is noteworthy because it associates spirituality with contributing to society, transcending our focus on ourselves and developing an outward-oriented worldview.

To summarize, the soul is the non-physical entity endowed with qualities such as kindness and love, which, coupled with our physical bodies, make us human. Spirituality encompasses our relationship to a higher power or universe, our capacity to transcend some human tendencies and manifest others and our ability to contribute to society.

At this point, you might be wondering if there is a relationship between spirituality and religion. Religion, which is a particular system of faith or worship, is different from spirituality, although they are often related and people can use the practice of their chosen religion to develop their spirituality. The major world religions are in agreement that spirituality is a universal human capacity, although how spirituality is expressed differs across faiths and cultures.[9] We can think of religion as providing a framework for the expression of our spirituality. Through teachings on the existence of a higher power, the importance of spiritual practices like prayer, the value of good deeds and the continued existence of the soul after the physical body dies, religion can teach us about patterns of thought and action that nurture our spiritual growth.

What about Source?

We cannot, of course, fully explore matters of the soul and spirituality without discussing the idea of the existence of a consciousness, a higher power or God that is greater than we are. We also cannot ignore the fact that there is much skepticism about the notion of God and doubt about whether God even exists. This doubt and the questions that arise from it are an important and valid part of a spiritual journey. Growth of any kind entails welcoming all the questions and doubts we have, and actively engaging in the journey of discovering the answers. It is only when we do not pursue answers to our questions that we cease to grow.

As we consider the idea of Source, we might also find ourselves wondering how to relate to a force or entity that defies definition. The truth is that if there is a force that gave rise to us, it would be beyond our comprehension. To better grasp how impossible it would be for us to understand any force or being that created us, let us think about the relationship between a sculptor who works with stone and a statue that she carves. Obviously the sculptor has intimate knowledge of the statue and all its intricacies, but the statue simply does not have the capacity to know anything about the sculptor. If we as human beings have been made or designed by a force greater than us, then just as the statue has no concept of the sculptor, our minds do not have the capacity to understand what brought us into being. To take this analogy even further, we can also say that the statue tells us something about the sculptor, but the statue does not and cannot tell us everything about the sculptor.

Needless to say, we have the freedom to define any higher power that brought us into being however we wish, whether it is in the language we use at our places of worship or when we commune with nature. I remember when my daughter was young, we noticed that her God was female. There are many cultures which have female deities, but it was fascinating to us because in our family we spoke of God as an unknowable essence, and it seemed special to both my husband and me that our daughter referred to God as "She." We decided to preserve this for her as long as we could, knowing that in much of the world God is referred to in the masculine. My daughter was six years old the last time I remember her referring to her female God. We do not know how she came to think of God as female, but it still warms my heart when I consider how empowering it must have been in her early years to understand the source of all things as feminine.

Our society's focus on empirical science has perhaps made us uncomfortable with the idea that there are things we do not fully understand that impact our lives. However, this is the territory we are in when we consider Source, our souls and our spirituality. Spirituality is that mystical feeling of connection between our souls and the force that gave rise to our being.

Integrating Spirituality and Mental Health

Data on the connection between mental health and spirituality is accumulating. The evidence is also mounting that human beings who acknowledge and nurture their spirituality increase their potential for mental wellness,[10,11] and that patient outcomes are improved when spirituality is addressed as a dimension of therapy.[12] As our knowledge about the connections between our spirituality and our mental health expands, we women need to expand our own awareness of who we are and become proactive in understanding and developing our spiritual capacities—the capacities of our souls. I have yet to meet a client who comes into my office anticipating that some of the dilemmas they are in have something to do with their soul or their spiritual life. Somehow we expect to be mentally and physically well, thrive and flourish without acknowledging the core of who we are—our souls.

When we do not address spirituality in attending to our mental health issues and the other concerns of our lives, we stand to lose considerably. The mental distress experienced by most women relates to the messages we have absorbed from birth about who we are and what our value is in a social context shaped by centuries of global oppression. When society, our communities and our families have devalued our existence, maintained systems of oppression and imposed impossible standards for us to live up to, is it any wonder we are struggling as much as we are? Clinical psychologists Dr. Margo Maine and Dr. Douglas Bunnell argue that

> "The media's objectification and sexualization of the female body has a lasting impact, persistently pressuring girls and women to assume an external view of themselves and their value as people. In turn, they are less able to identify, express, process, or respect their emotions, thoughts and instincts. Messages from the outside eclipse any inner life."[13]

Understanding the social context within which we exist as women is an important first step in our journey to reclaim our birthright as noble souls. When we ask ourselves with loving and open curiosity why we see or do things the way we do, or why we think a certain way, we can begin to access and identify the false messages we have absorbed from the world. As we bring into awareness all the beliefs we hold about ourselves, we can begin to let go of those that no longer serve us well.

Seeing ourselves as spiritual beings and understanding the extent to which spirituality can transform our well-being and mental health is liberating. We need to fully engage in learning about our spiritual nature, and use the insights we gain to foster our spiritual growth. The compartmentalization of our existence, or the separation of our mental well-being from our spiritual and physical well-being, is one of the key challenges we need to overcome to support our own development. True growth is only possible through the integration of all our capacities and the recognition that we are made up of both the physical and the spiritual. We cannot make complete sense of life, and feel balanced and whole, without acknowledging what makes us human—the soul.

To change the trajectory of our lives for ourselves and all who come after us we need to integrate all our different dimensions. We need to get to the heart of how we define ourselves, consider what gives us true value and learn to navigate life with conscious knowledge of our true identity. We need to live our lives fully aware that we are noble souls.

Becoming Spiritually Minded

So what would it look like if we acknowledged that some of our mental distress might have spiritual foundations, and we addressed the root causes of our angst? What if we saw that our anxiety, depression, feelings of worthlessness and drive to be perfect and meet unrealistic standards as symptoms that we have forgotten who we are at a spiritual level?

From what I see in my practice, women who are open to thinking about themselves as spiritual beings, or at least open to acknowledging that there is more to their lives than their physical existence, make greater progress in therapy and heal faster. They also tend to move more quickly toward the integration of different aspects of themselves, and they begin to navigate life in a way that honors their own sacred nature and that of those around them. This is particularly true for women who have survived any kind of trauma, and who understand that their soul remains whole regardless of the tragedies they have endured.

As we have seen, the data indicate that making room for our spirituality will enhance our mental health and well-being. When we begin to understand ourselves as spiritual beings and draw on the capacities of our souls, we open the door to our own thriving. There is great peace that comes from knowing who we really are: seeing ourselves as worthy not because of what we do, but because of the essence of who we are as souls. We must, therefore, support ourselves to move in the direction of having a more accurate awareness of our spiritual identity. Having the conscious knowledge that we are spiritual beings allows us to embark on a journey of spiritual growth in which we intentionally increase our self-awareness, strive to transcend our lower tendencies and develop spiritually through habits such as prayer, meditation and mindfulness.

The impact of cultivating our spirituality will also extend beyond our own lives. When we start seeing ourselves as noble souls, we will also see those around us as noble souls on their own spiritual journeys. We will be in a position to imbue our daughters, sons and everyone we mentor with the understanding that they too are noble souls, and we will be able to nurture them in ways that support the growth and development of their spiritual capacities.

The journey of spiritual growth requires that we understand, to the extent that we can, the nature of the soul and our capacities as spiritual beings. Once we have a sense of who we are, we need to live our lives and make choices that align with our spiritual nature and facilitate our spiritual growth. We also need to know how to navigate the world and its challenges from our true nature as noble souls, and not from the lies we have absorbed about our value and our identity. This is the journey you are being invited to take in this book. Together we will increase our understanding of our souls, and explore ways to navigate our lives to enhance our spiritual growth. We will learn how to understand the day-to-day joys and concerns of our lives from the perspective of spirit. We will also come to see the world as the workshop for our spiritual growth. As we grow spiritually, we will see ourselves as agents of change and positive contributors to others' welfare. We will become spiritually minded.

As her therapy progressed, my client Sonia was able to ask herself, with a gentle curiosity, questions about how a worldview that placed such a high value on body weight was serving her. She began to see herself as a victim of societal messages that held her to unrealistic standards, and got relief from clearing the memories of being teased in elementary school. Sonia also took stock of the unique qualities of her soul, including determination and creativity, and her healing journey continues.

Before we contemplate the qualities of our souls and how to grow spiritually, let us first take a look at what it means to navigate life as women.

Recollections: Circles of Connection

The afternoon sun beats down relentlessly as I drive through the dusty Amboseli plains. To collect data for my doctoral research, I am looking for a family unit of elephants that spends time outside the national park. As I pass a Maasai settlement I see a group of women in the sparse shade of an acacia tree. With time I come to think of these gatherings as circles of connection: groups of Maasai women with their clean-shaven heads, ornate jewelry and colorful robes gathering together to work on their bead crafts, talking while waving their hands and baring their teeth in laughter. Their daily tasks of tending to the home and getting water are done for the day, and their delight in being together is so palpable that I long to be one of them and to understand what gives rise to the mirth. Their bonds with one another seem deep and loving, and it intrigues me that these circles of friendship and happiness exist side by side with the challenges of having little access to education and few rights as women. So begins my curiosity about the feminine, and what it means to be a woman.

Many years later I carry these reflections with me to the United Arab Emirates, where women's circles of connection take on a different yet similar form. In the privacy of their homes, my friends take off their black hijab revealing elegant clothes, stunning makeup and, again, the relaxed pleasure of friendship. Sometimes the gatherings turn into spontaneous dances, with children joining in. While pondering the contrast between these women's reserved and covered public demeanor and their playful gaiety when in one another's company in private spaces, I think again about the power of women.

As a mother in my forties, I get yet another glimpse into the gifts of the feminine when, in snowy New England, my neighbors brave the weather to gather for our monthly book club. As busy women who work both outside and inside the home, we welcome the chance to sit and be still and we sigh with contentment at the offer of hot tea. We do not laugh with the same abandon as Maasai women and we have yet to break into spontaneous dance, but we are joyful and earnest in our discussion of the book, our children and the state of the world. We support each other through the loss of parents and illnesses, we eat copious amounts of chocolate, we watch each other's children grow and we revel in the opportunity to be together.

It is hard to express the gratitude I feel for all the women across the globe who have taught me about the power and possibility of the feminine. Through them I learned that regardless of our circumstances, we women bring wisdom and keen insight to our endeavors. We courageously change the world in both big and small ways, and we are deeply committed to nurturing our families and those around us. We are also particularly skilled at building bridges of friendship and authentic connection, and we do all this in a world that has yet to fully recognize the gifts of the feminine.

CHAPTER 2

What Does It Mean
to Be a Woman?

"My upbringing was challenging to say the least. My mother always told me she would rather have had a son. At one point she told me that she only had two children because her first child was not a boy."

May and I were having coffee in Abu Dhabi and telling one another our stories. She had been recruited from Canada to work as a counselor at a college on the outskirts of the city, and we met at the school our children attended.

"Whoa! Our stories are similar, although I think in your culture the preference for males is expressed more directly," I replied.

"Oh, yes! My mother still has no problem telling me what a disappointment I am."

"And yet you and I would never dream of saying such things to our girls," I replied, thinking of our daughters who as second graders were both feisty members of the school swimming team.

"Don't you think it is amazing, when you look at history, that our generation is changing so much? I hear my grandmother talk to my mother, and it's the same story—you should have been a boy. It's been going on for centuries and then, in one generation, we get to stop the cycle." May snapped her fingers for emphasis.

This shift in our regard for women is one I see both in my social circles and in the course of my work. I am humbled by our capacity as women to both individually and collectively shift ancient patterns of thought and behavior that have prevented us from understanding our true value and fulfilling our potential. We are already effecting great changes and we will continue to do so to the extent that we draw deeply from our gifts as women and reject patriarchal norms.

The Patriarchy Isn't Really Working for Us

Perhaps the most significant challenge to moving forward as women is that the social context within which we exist is, for the most part, a patriarchal system in which men are considered more valuable than women. Activist and author bell hooks states in her book *The Will to Change: Men, Masculinity, and Love* that "Patriarchy is a political-social system that insists that males are inherently dominating, superior to everything and everyone deemed weak, especially females, and endowed with the right to dominate and rule over the weak . . . "[1] As such, patriarchy upholds the seeking of control and power, competition, winning, and male privilege as some of its core values.[2,3,4]

Being born into an environment where males are explicitly or implicitly considered more valuable than females has a profound effect on women. Recognizing at a deep level that we are not welcomed as we are, and that we are considered "less than" even before our journeys in life begin, we either struggle to survive or we adapt ourselves to fit into a society that at best ignores our needs and at worst violates us. Throughout history, women of all backgrounds have been subjected to discrimination, physical abuse and sexual violence, and these negative impacts on women's lives are compounded by other forces of oppression such as racism, casteism, tribalism, homophobia and ableism. When the pressures placed on women prove too great, many of us shut down. Mental health statistics alert us to the deep angst of the feminine: women are nearly twice as likely as men to be diagnosed with depression;[5] lifetime prevalence rates of anxiety disorders in women are higher than they are for men;[6] women are more likely to develop symptoms of PTSD;[7] and women are more likely to be diagnosed with eating disorders.[8] The explanations offered for these phenomena include differences in socioeconomics; access to resources, power and control over life circumstances; and gender differences in physiology and hormonal makeup.[9] They also reflect the challenges of being female in a world that has not yet truly welcomed women.

Navigating such a world has also meant many of us have become vulnerable to the notion that our value must be earned. We have therefore adopted different strategies for seeking value: some of us strive for perfection and define ourselves by our accomplishments, some of us put ourselves under great pressure to be the best at everything while at the same time feeling like we are never good enough, and some of us acquiesce to our fate and decide there is no need to show up as all that we can be. Whatever strategy we choose for surviving, we are generally pulled away from the core of our being as noble souls. We lose sight of who we really are and what we can contribute to society.

In the paperwork my clients fill out before their first appointment, I ask them to list their strengths. So far, all my clients who identify as male list at least two or three strengths. Sadly, this is not the case with clients who identify as female.

Take Keisha, for example. As we began her first session, I noticed she had not answered the question.

"So what would you say your strengths are?" I prompted gently

"Well, I don't really have any."

I made a mental note that this would be an area to address with her in the course of therapy. I also felt sad that as a society we have let Keisha down and not reflected her strengths back to her enough for her to internalize them.

I wish I could say a client telling me they have no strengths is a rare occurrence, but it is not. Women of all ages and backgrounds have told me they do not have any strengths or they do not know what their strengths are, even though they are nurses, teachers, entrepreneurs, artists, musicians, lawyers, doctors, high-achieving athletes and successful high school and college students.

There are a number of reasons seemingly successful women are reluctant to acknowledge their strengths. Maureen Murdock, author of *The Heroine's Journey* writes that "Because society denigrates feminine qualities, a woman is not likely to value herself as a woman. She is seen and sees herself as lacking and operates on the myth of inferiority."[10] In addition, women who have been successful in primarily masculine domains can feel empty and unfulfilled because their feminine strengths such as superior communication skills and the capacity to build consensus and harmonious relationships[11] were not fully factored into what made them successful. These women evaluate themselves by male-defined standards and "find themselves deficient or lacking in the qualities that men value."[12] They struggle because the patriarchy is not designed with the needs and qualities of the feminine in mind.

Thus far, much of the effort to address gender equality has been about women gaining equal rights or representation in domains designed by males for males, with the assumption that when women are equally represented in the top levels of government and management, we will have achieved equality.[13] The truth is women cannot truly flourish in a system that does not take into account their strengths and needs. To move forward, we will need to envision and put in place new ways of organizing ourselves as societies and communities that truly take into account the reality of all genders and foster the development of all. This process will, of course, need women to be clear on the needs of the feminine because in our struggle to survive in the patriarchy, we have sometimes lost sight of what the feminine has to offer. To manifest all that women bring, we will need to connect with our spiritual nature at the deepest level and uphold our needs with integrity. We must connect with our souls.

Soul Calling Earth

When I think about being a woman, my mind strangely conjures up the image of being on a vessel floating in outer space. I see myself as an alien among many on the spaceship waiting to beam down to Earth to learn about life there. A computer generates a randomly selected combination of factors which will influence my experience on Earth: the geographical location where I arrive, my ethnicity, race, economic situation, genetics, aptitudes and gender. My fellow aliens also receive their assignments, and when each of us is ready we begin the process of beaming down to Earth to find the perfect womb in which to start our learning experience. While there we all know that even though we have been assigned different experiences, we are just visiting to learn about human existence.

I share these odd workings of my imagination because I believe they reflect some truth about being human souls on Planet Earth. Where we are born, our family, our community, our race, our ability, our economic situation and our gender all inform our experience, but they are not our essential nature—our souls are. The circumstances we find ourselves in influence the experience we have on the planet, but they are not the core of our identity—they do not define us.

The perspective that our souls have no gender, and take on gender to have a particular experience, opens us to a very liberating understanding of what it means to be a woman. We know our souls to be our core identity and we understand our experience on the planet as female as just that—an experience. It is one that comes with particular points of view, capacities and, of course, many gifts. The experience of being female also influences the joys and trials we encounter, but it does not define who we are at our core.

Seeing ourselves as souls experiencing life on Earth as female also allows us to reject the labels and attitudes that have been placed on women that have nothing to do with the truth of who we are, and enables us to claim our rightful place in society. Most importantly, we can pursue justice and demand equal rights with a deep knowledge that the human soul is the same regardless of the gender of the individual. Understanding that at the core all human beings are souls also helps us see through any mystique around men that the patriarchy has created. As we acknowledge ourselves as souls having a female experience, we will see non-binary individuals as souls having a non-binary experience, and men as souls having a male experience. We will also begin to understand that the ascendancy men have enjoyed throughout history is the result of the privilege and opportunity they have been granted in a system they created to maintain power. It is interesting that our language already reflects the equality of our souls: the powerful attributes in each of us are not dependent on gender. We admire courage, kindness and generosity. There is no such thing as female kindness, non-binary kindness or male kindness. These attributes are the standard of excellence of every human being regardless of gender.

Starting to see ourselves as souls not only changes how we think of our gender, but it also invites us to revisit the other narratives we hold about who we are. We know that as human beings we derive a sense of self from our membership in social groups and the value and meaning we attach to the groups to which we belong.[14] Many of us live at the intersection of a number of social identities which include our gender, race, religion, ethnicity, political affiliation, age, sexual identity, interests, nationality, social class, economic and health status.[15] How, then, do we reconcile the idea that our true nature as spiritual beings stems from our souls with the social identities that affect our lives in such significant ways? A helpful perspective is to consider our spiritual essence as our primary identity and all of our social identities as secondary. Our primary identity—the soul—makes us human. Our secondary identities are then the factors that determine our experience on earth: where we are born, where we live, our race, our ethnicity and our gender. The multiple secondary identities we carry—while shaping our experiences—do not change the essence of who we are. As souls, we tap into our full potential and power when we reject the idea that our secondary identities define who we are, and see them instead as the determinants of the experiences we have on this planet where our purpose is to foster the growth of who we are at the level of our primary identity.

Differentiating between our primary and secondary identities does not mean we tolerate injustice and the systems that uphold it. Instead, we approach the pursuit of justice for all on the premise that we are all human souls. Having our soul as our primary identity means we reject the idea that we are fundamentally different from one another, and instead start to embrace our common humanity. As author and journalist Isabel Wilkerson states in her book *Caste: The Origin of Our Discontents,* it is up to each of us "to determine for ourselves and to make the world see that what is inside of us—our beliefs and dreams, how we love and express that love, the things that we can actually control—is more important than the outward traits we had no say in."[16]

When we live with a conscious knowledge of both our primary and our secondary identities, we can see that there is no "them" and "us," there is only "us." I recognize, even as I write this, that as a global community we are a long way from upholding the dignity and well-being of all human beings, but the heart of moving forward in all the challenges we face around equality for all is the idea that we are, at the core, human souls.

Creating clarity around the difference between primary and secondary identity does not mean we do not acknowledge and celebrate the rich diversity of the human experience: each of us enhances the whole when we express all we bring from our multiple secondary identities. Recognizing that we all share a common primary identity, the human soul, becomes the foundation for respecting and celebrating the diversity that people with different secondary identities bring to the human experience. We appreciate diversity of point of view and life experience, and yet understand that at our core we are all the same. When we view our secondary identities as determining experience, but not as part of our core identity, we become free to explore the experiences that come with any particular secondary identity without the burden of having it define us. As women, we recognize our gender allows each of us to contribute something valuable and unique to society, but we also know all human beings are simply noble souls.

The Gifts of the Feminine

Some years ago I was in a workshop where the presenter asked the audience what bothered us most about the state of the world. My answer came immediately: it pains me deeply that many of the women I meet do not know their value. Many of us feel tarnished by our experiences of physical abuse and sexual trauma, and some of us feel we have been robbed of our sense of personhood by the forces of societal oppression. I still remember one of my clients shrugging casually as she told me about the abusive relationship she was in, "I've been sexually abused by the men in my family since I was four, so now it is the only way I know how to relate to men."

Some of us have lost sight of ourselves and fallen victim to aggressively materialistic messages that foster insecurity to generate income for multi-million dollar businesses. As one of my clients started to discern the damaging content of the social messages about ideal body type, perfect physical appearance and popularity which barrage women in modern Western culture, she insightfully commented that "the ads are designed to make me unhappy with who I am, so that I keep buying stuff to fix the unhappy."

To change these patterns of self-loathing and discontent, we must become consciously aware of our souls. We need to know that we have our most important resource for navigating life at the very core of our being, and that our true value and our power comes from there. It is our own deep inner work that will support us to change patterns of thought and behavior that have been developed in a world unprepared to welcome us as we are. When we view gender as experience we become free to explore dimensions of that experience without burden. We do not see ourselves as less than or inherently deficient because we came to experience life on earth as female. We become free to inhabit the full reality of the feminine and all its gifts. We dare, as author Kathie Carlson puts it, to "imagine ourselves whole."[17]

So what are the gifts of the feminine? What must those of us who experience life as females know, acknowledge and manifest to reach our fullest potential? What do women know that must be shared for the whole of humanity to realize its destiny?

Some of the gifts of the feminine appear to be rooted in biology. Dr. Louann Brizendine, neuropsychiatrist and author of *The Female Brain*, writes, "The female brain has tremendous unique aptitudes—outstanding verbal agility, the ability to connect deeply in friendship, a nearly psychic capacity for reading faces and tone of voice for emotions and states of mind, and the ability to diffuse conflict. All of this is hardwired into the brains of women. These are the talents women are born with that many men, frankly, are not."[18] Dr. Brizendine goes on to state that the way particular brain structures in the female embryo develop results in females valuing and having greater facility with "communication, connection, emotional sensitivity and responsiveness."[19]

Throughout history women have shown boldness and courage in ways that have allowed all of human society to evolve. Rosa Parks's refusal to give up her seat on a bus for a white passenger in Alabama was an act of moral courage and a key moment in the Civil Rights Movement. Founder of the Green Belt Movement and Nobel Peace Laureate Wangarĩ Maathai fought to combat deforestation by encouraging women to plant trees, and also opposed development in green spaces in the city of Nairobi despite political opposition. In her memoir *Unbound: My Story of Liberation and the Birth of the Me Too Movement,* Tarana Burke, activist and founder of the Me Too movement against sexual abuse and sexual harassment, tells a story of great resilience and courage.[20] In this kind of moral leadership, women have and will continue to be contributors to world peace.

Understanding gender as experience rather than identity also allows us to see that each vantage point brings perspectives that are important for everyone's progress. Authors of *Female Authority,* Polly Young-Eisendrath and Florence Wiedemann, write, "the woman must claim her femininity as worthwhile . . . This means that the woman comes to recognize her contribution to culture and society as intrinsically valuable in whatever feminine form it has taken: greater empathic skill in relationship, a strong and reliable aesthetic orientation, an altruistic desire to provide care, etc. Through this kind of self-regard, the woman is finally able to form an equal partnership with men."[21]

When we see our gender as experience, we get to express the qualities of the feminine including our capacity to connect with others, our emotional intelligence, our keen intuition, our aptitude for nuanced and clear communication and our moral courage. We can also appreciate the gifts of other vantage points without associating them with more meaning or value than they deserve.

At no point in history has the opportunity for souls to thrive regardless of gender been as great as it is now. Obviously, women's accomplishments are too numerous to list here, and we have many examples which demonstrate that women make significant contributions in all kinds of service to humanity; they are at the forefront of tackling many challenges facing society and they have also risen to the highest positions of leadership across the globe.

Opportunities for women to thrive will continue to unfold as we increase access to education, resources and opportunity. We will also shift the status of the feminine on the planet to the extent that we connect with the deep well of power in our souls; the tools and concepts presented in this book will help us with this. Our true excellence lies in the development of our spiritual qualities. Just as my friend May moved through life with determination, courage and the insight to effect a social revolution by protecting her daughter from demeaning family messages, we all need to draw on our well of spiritual qualities to move ourselves and our world forward. Let us now further explore the core of our reality as souls. To quote Maya Angelou's soulful celebration of the gifts of the feminine, this is the time for each of us to see ourselves as a "phenomenal woman."[22]

PART TWO

Keys to Spiritual Growth

Recollections: Seeking Worthiness, Discovering Nobility

I am 12 and sitting on the branch of a large loquat tree when I see my aunt's car come down the driveway. I scamper to greet her, hoping that my cousins are also in the car. Rubbing leaves and bark off the brown floral dress I am wearing, I run oblivious of the sharp gravel under my bare feet, eager to give our most respectful greeting for elders to this aunt I adore. She acknowledges me with, "Marhaba, Kadzo. Wow! You have really gained weight!" I feel crushed and wish I could disappear, but instead I look down awkwardly, trying to smile. I know this is not a value-free observation, because I have heard many conversations between the women of my family in which my mother is complimented for how thin she is. My cousins come out of the car and together we look for ripe loquats, eating the yellow flesh, spitting out the brown seeds and pursing our lips at the fruit's tartness. That evening, I stand before the mirror in my bedroom looking critically at my body with a sad feeling that I do not look how I am supposed to.

Of course, I now know my body was right on cue, developing exactly as it should have been at 12. Although much time has passed, this interaction with my aunt is as clear in my mind as if it happened yesterday, and I see how it contributed to many years of feeling inadequate and seeking

49

worthiness by dieting and putting unnecessary pressure on myself to do everything well.

Eighteen years later, I am standing at the kitchen sink in our small apartment in Columbus, Ohio, washing dishes and absently staring out the window. Tears stream down my face to join the warm, soapy dishwater. My husband walks in, offers to do the dishes instead of me and notices the tears. He asks why I am crying and in doing so unleashes a flood of emotion in me. "I don't even have a business card," I whisper as the tears keep flowing. He kindly offers that I am the CEO of our household, but that does not cut it. His compassion does not make up for how disempowered I feel in my new life.

These days, I think of those early years of our marriage as the dark years. I met my husband in Nairobi and we moved from Kenya to the United States so he could complete his education. I had left my family, a promising career, my country and all that I was familiar with to follow a guy who was never home because of his training. All the markers of worthiness—my paycheck, my status as a conservation professional, the expertise I offered at meetings and conferences—were gone and although I did not recognize it at the time, I was depressed and lonely.

Five years later I am sitting in a doctor's office in Dubai. He speaks gently, but the words are jarring, "The next test we would do to determine if the spots on your brain MRI are signs of multiple sclerosis is a spinal tap." My mind immediately goes to my five-year-old son and three-year-

old daughter. I ask myself what having this illness would mean for them. I feel simultaneously terrified and hopeful that all will be well.

A dear friend calls me to say hello, and I tell her about the progressive numbing on the right side of my body, and about the CAT scans and MRIs that have so far yielded little information about what is going on. She recommends I contact healer Julie Burns Walker to get a different perspective. It takes some weeks to get an appointment, but I finally talk to Julie on the phone. I tell her about my physical symptoms and also about my struggle with worthlessness and feeling that I lost my career. Julie responds with words that change my life, "If you could see yourself as I see you, none of that would matter. I see your attributes—your sincerity and your passion for truth. Yes, if you could see that, the rest wouldn't matter at all." In that moment, I feel truly seen. It is as if my soul understands something important when it is acknowledged for being sincere and truthful. Julie offers me very useful advice to address my physical symptoms, but more significantly she gives me my first invitation to recognize the attributes of my soul. I know in my gut that my view of myself has changed in a profound way.

Another 15 years have passed, and it is that precious time of morning when the light outside is soft and the house inside is quiet. I am sitting on our red couch with my cloth-covered prayer book on my lap. I reflect on the words I have just read about the Creator's love for me, and I realize I am beginning to relate to passages that made no sense to me some years ago. There was a time I could not imagine what it meant to be loved unconditionally by the Creator, but now I notice

there is a little shift and I see it is possible to be loved in this way. I also notice I have been holding space for the qualities my husband and others acknowledge in me and I am starting to see them as the noble qualities they are: gifts from the Creator to me.

CHAPTER 3

Mine Your Inner Gems

"I am such a mess, I can't even get a job. There's just nothing good about me," Nailah exclaimed tearfully as she shared her disappointment about being turned down for a job she really wanted. Nailah was a bright college student who had been seeing me for a few months for anxiety treatment.

"I get it," I said, pulling out a large pad of art paper and some colored pencils. I drew a large circle on a clean page and looked up into Nailah's puzzled eyes.

"Let's imagine for a minute that I met your mother. What are the things she would say about you? Remember, I'd be meeting her for the first time and people don't usually start with negative stuff when they realize they have a mutual connection. So what would your mom say about you?"

"She would say I am funny, and kind, and smart."

"Anything else?" I prompted as I wrote those words in large purple letters in the circle.

"She'd say I am hardworking."

"And what would your father say about you?"

"He'd say the same things, and he'd also say I'm determined. Mom might say I'm determined too."

I nodded as I wrote down newly mentioned attributes and underlined those that were already on the list.

"And what would your professors say about you?"

"They'd say I am responsible and hardworking."

"And how about your brother and sisters?"

"They'd say I am funny. Yes, funny and creative with games. I also help them with school projects."

"Anyone else in your life?"

"My grandparents and my boyfriend."

"What would they say?"

"The same things, mostly. My boyfriend would say I am fun to be around and a good listener."

"And how about your friends?"

"That I am kind and a good listener and I give them stuff."

"Okay. So, if I were to tell you that I want you to meet someone I know who is funny, kind, smart, hardworking, determined, helpful, responsible, creative, a good listener, fun to be around and generous, what would you say?"

"Yes, I'd want to meet them. They sound like fun."

"Well," I said as I turned the paper to face her. "This is you."

Nailah became quiet for a few moments, then I noticed her eyes were tearing up and she said, "I never realized that."

"Yes, this is you and these are your amazing qualities. Also, notice some of them are underlined several times, which means more than one person in your life sees the same qualities in you. Do you think all these people met and decided on a game plan of what to say in case they meet someone who asks about you?"

"No, no, they didn't," Nailah laughed.

"So take this home and make a big poster for yourself."

I offered her the sheet of paper which she received smiling, and took a few moments to look at it again.

At her appointment the following week, Nailah showed me a photograph of a colorful poster she had made with the words that described her attributes decorated with whimsical flowers and trees and said, "It helps me so much when I look at it."

As a therapist, I have noticed that how clients define themselves is key to their capacity to make progress. Yet in our materialistic society which prizes accomplishments and outward appearance, few of us think of ourselves in terms of our character's qualities, and even fewer of us recognize these qualities as attributes of our souls. In this chapter we will discuss the attributes of our souls, and learn how to mine these inner gems. As we embark on this journey of learning, it is important to note we are entering a zone of paradox. The soul is indeed a mysterious entity that defies definition and can never be fully comprehended, and yet we get our best shot at life and grow to our full potential when we have an awareness of our spiritual nature and the internal dynamics that make us human. While we cannot know everything about the soul, learning as much as we can is in our best interest and supports us to live more meaningfully.

The intervention I used with Nailah, which I have come to call an attributes inventory, is a powerful tool for inviting people to begin recognizing their qualities or attributes. You may have noticed I did not ask Nailah how she would describe herself. This is partly because mental distress typically arises from the fact that we do not see ourselves as we really are. By asking Nailah about how others see her, I bypassed any blocks she may have had to seeing herself accurately, and accessed how she thinks she is experienced by others. This then allowed her to take in the information about herself.

Not So Black Box

When asked about the nature of our souls, most of us do not know what to say. We often consider our inner-most selves as some kind of black box that we have little information about, and the internal workings of which we cannot understand. We generally go about our lives ignoring our inner reality and disconnected from the core of our existence, then we wonder why we live in an age of widespread mental distress. We have, for the most part, responded to the challenge of not being able to fully comprehend our inner reality by ignoring our soul and living lives uninformed by its needs.

It took just a few simple questions to get Nailah to develop a list of her attributes, and she was moved to tears by the simple yet profound reminder that she is experienced by others through these qualities. Nailah was quick to embrace a different view of herself at the age of 23, but what if Nailah, or any of us, was offered a framework in childhood to understand that the soul has specific qualities? How different would life be if, at an early age, we were introduced to a rich vocabulary of all our soul's attributes?

If we really knew who we were, and were called to the attributes of our souls from infancy, we would be more content and grounded human beings. We would understand ourselves based on our true reality, and we would be less susceptible to the sway of materialistic demands to be perfect: to have perfect careers, bodies, homes and social connections. This chapter explores our attributes and provides the information we need to support the growth of our souls.

How Do We Know about the Soul?

Where does the information we have about the soul come from? There are two primary sources of knowledge we can draw on to learn more about our souls: science and spiritual traditions. We can look to spiritual traditions as a source of knowledge about our soul and we can learn about its capacities through science. These two ways of knowing, while often pitted against each other, are both valid paths to deeper understanding and knowledge about the world and about who we are.

The revealed religions of the world all provide a vision for what is possible for us, and they address how human beings can grow spiritually. You may be wondering why I am speaking about the world's religions as a whole. If we examine the teachings that pertain to the growth of our inner essence, we find the world's religions are far more similar than they are different. Every religion has its form of the Golden Rule which, in stipulating that each of us, "do unto others as you would have them do unto you," provides a blueprint for both individual spiritual development and social cohesion. All faiths teach us to be kind and to look out for one another. All faiths encourage us to be forgiving and overlook the faults of those around us. These core teachings give us most of the information we have about our souls. From the world's spiritual traditions we know the soul is what gives human beings consciousness, it is what makes each of us unique, it is the part of us that reflects attributes such as kindness, love and generosity and it is the part of us that longs for connection with its Source.

As we discussed in the Introduction, we know human beings thrive when they manifest their soul's capacity for connection, service and generosity. Psychology, in particular, has pointed us in the direction of recognizing the existence of an inner dimension to human existence. Carl Jung, one of the founders of modern psychology, taught that our ability to think, dream and imagine are capacities of the soul.[1] Psychotherapist Sarah Krakauer tells us that "every individual, no matter how damaged and fragmented, has an inner core that, once potentiated, can guide the individual to a state of harmonious functioning."[2] When working with clients in emotional turmoil, Dr. Jon Connelly, the developer of Rapid Resolution Therapy, a modality which uses multilevel communication to resolve emotional disturbance and maladaptive behavior rapidly and painlessly, invites them to think that, "the peace, excitement, clarity and wisdom at your center is who you are."[3]

The Attributes

The attributes I brought to Nailah's attention are part of what makes us human and also what makes each of us unique. These are the qualities of the soul, the building blocks of who we are. Linda Kavelin Popov, founder of The Virtues Project, a global initiative which seeks to inspire people to use virtues in their daily lives, defines these attributes as, "the essence of soulfulness. They are a great mystery because they are both within us and beyond us. They are described by all cultures and religions as the qualities of the Divinity and the simple elements of the human soul."[4]

The significant role the attributes play in our lives is, not surprisingly, acknowledged in the field of mental health. For example, Richard Schwartz, founder of Internal Family Systems therapy, considers attributes as part of the essential self and states that following a great loss or traumatic event he supports his clients to access, "*the Self*—an essence of calm, clarity, compassion, and connectedness."[5] There are many more attributes that we are familiar with, such as kindness, generosity, truthfulness, friendliness and caring: it would be impossible to have an exhaustive list of all the attributes of the soul. However, learning what we can of this vocabulary will be useful in fostering our soul's growth. (See Figure 1 for a list of some attributes of the soul.) Kavelin Popov and her colleagues on The Virtues Project have made a tremendous contribution to the conversation about the attributes of our souls and how to cultivate them in ourselves and others.[6]

When we learn to recognize these qualities in ourselves, we are noticing the attributes of our own souls, and when we recognize them in others, we are noticing the attributes of their souls. When we are kind or loving or generous or determined, we are expressing attributes of the soul. We can think of these attributes as a reflection of the Divine in each of us. In all spiritual traditions, the Creator or a Higher Power is described as loving, merciful, truthful, generous and gracious. In Islam, God is believed to have ninety-nine names, each of which describe his attributes: The Merciful, The Gentle, The Ever-Forgiving.[7] The Jewish tradition invokes Thirteen Attributes of Mercy in asking for God's compassion and forgiveness.[8] The Christian Beatitudes are blessings to those who manifest attributes including mercy, meekness and purity of heart,[9] while the second letter of Peter in the New Testamant encourages the development of love, kindness and fortitude.[10] As human beings, we reflect an aspect of the Divine when we show any of these attributes. The idea that human beings are made in the image of God, as stated in The Old Testament,[11] is the idea that we have the potential to reflect God's attributes, and that the noble qualities of the Divine are also in us. The developers of The Oneness Model on human development and evolution, Julie Burns Walker and Deborah Christensen, call our attributes our "inner treasury of the Creator's gems."[12]

Assertiveness	Excellence	Loyalty
Caring	Friendliness	Patience
Cheerfulness	Generosity	Resilience
Consideration	Gratitude	Respect
Compassion	Honesty	Responsibility
Courage	Humility	Self-Discipline
Courtesy	Humor	Strength
Determination	Joyfulness	Thoughtfulness
Empathy	Kindness	Truthfulness
Enthusiasm	Love	Wisdom

Figure 1: *Some Attributes of the Soul*

Way beyond Skills

We cannot overemphasize the importance of understanding our attributes as qualities of the soul. We live in a world that would have us believe some of these qualities are skills that can be learned, but this does not reflect the fullness of what they are. Yes, with practice we can train ourselves to act kindly, but in doing so we are not learning a skill in the same way we would learn how to write calligraphy or play a musical instrument through regular practice. What we are actually doing is expressing and developing an aspect of our true nature. The attributes are the spiritual qualities we have been endowed with, and by becoming aware of them and consciously cultivating their growth, we are mining the gems that are already within; we are developing our birthright as human beings. There is a qualitative difference between thinking of kindness as a skill we use and understanding that by expressing the attribute of kindness, we are manifesting an attribute of our soul. Acknowledging our attributes gives us power: if we lived with a conscious awareness of all the attributes we hold in our souls, nothing could keep us down. We would know ourselves as noble souls because of the rich repository of attributes within.

Attributes as Protection

You may recall my client Sonia from Chapter 1, who had been teased about her body size in elementary school and was struggling with an eating disorder at seventeen. What if, by the time Sonia was encountering the third-grade bully, she already had an understanding of herself that was broader and deeper than her physical body? What if, from the time she was born, she received a clear message that she is a noble soul with wonderful attributes, and it was these attributes that defined her? What if, as she was growing up, Sonia was acknowledged for being kind on the playground, generous for sharing her toys and determined when she completed challenging homework? And what if she was told that kindness, generosity and determination were attributes of her soul? Then, perhaps, she would be able to look that bully in the eye and say, "That's not true. My body does not define who I am." Or at the very least, she may have been able to shrug off the hurtful words because they contained no truth about who she was and the potential she held.

Every day in my work, I meet with women whose self-concept has been defined negatively through messages from social media and advertising. The protective value of teaching children and young people about their attributes and planting the seeds of a definition of self that transcends physical appearance, social popularity and accomplishments cannot be overstated. Understanding ourselves at the level of the soul and its attributes protects and buffers us from many of the negative forces at play in the world.

Attributes Are the Substance of Human Interaction

Just as our attributes are the foundational building blocks of who we are as people, they are also the means through which we experience one another—the substance of human relationships. We can easily name people who demonstrate the attribute of helpfulness, and we can also name a few who have shown great courage.

As a clinician, I learned a lot about the power of thinking about the attributes of the people around us through my client Petra. Unlike Nailah, Petra was not as open to acknowledging that she had inner gifts, and vehemently rejected the idea that there was anything positive about her. I attempted to engage her in doing an attributes inventory, but she did not want to participate in any activity that associated her with anything positive. I felt deep compassion for Petra and I admired her capacity to do so much for others despite the pain she was in. I also felt myself internally scratching my head about what to do as I sat across the room from her. Thankfully, I was inspired to take a less direct route.

I ventured tentatively, "Tell me about your daughter."

Petra's demeanor softened, and she readily described her daughter in terms of her attributes. "She is kind and open-hearted. She really wants to do good in the world and she is a deep thinker—very smart."

"She sounds lovely."

I asked Petra to tell me about her closest friend. Again she responded as I thought she would.

"She is warm and funny, and always ready to help. She is also very protective of me."

"Notice how you experience these people you love—it is through their qualities, right? So how do you think they experience you?"

"Well, my friends also say I am funny, caring and a good mother," Petra smiled.

It was heartwarming to see how, through considering how she experiences others, Petra was able to name the qualities I had already begun to see in her in our sessions together, despite her initially rejecting the idea.

How, then, do we cultivate our soul's growth and connect with our attributes in deep and meaningful ways? The most important factor in fostering this is our conscious engagement with the process. Our souls grow from the intentional cultivation of our attributes. When we are actively examining and assessing our inner reality, we grow faster than when we are moving unconsciously through life unaware of how we are doing and how we are affecting those around us.

Just as my client Nailah was moved to tears as she saw herself for the first time as a repository of all her

wonderful attributes, let us each take stock of and cultivate the attributes of our souls. Let us mine all our inner
gems with love and gentle encouragement, and claim our
birthright as noble souls.

To continue our journey of spiritual growth, in the next
chapter we will look at how human nature influences the
development of our souls.

TO GO DEEPER

*Growing Our Attributes—
Mining Our Inner Gems*

Here are four steps and some questions for reflection to support you with cultivating your attributes and growing spiritually:

1. ACKNOWLEDGE OUR ATTRIBUTES

We need to develop an awareness of the attributes and start to notice them in ourselves and others. Begin by creating your own attributes inventory. You will need a notebook and the list of attributes provided in Figure 1. First, write down the names of four or five people you are closest to and list the attributes they would use to describe you next to each name. Do not be concerned about repeated attributes, as they indicate how you are consistently experienced by those around you. Next, list the names of co-workers, supervisors, teachers, coaches or anyone you interact with, and write down the attributes they would describe you with. Finally, transfer all the attributes you have listed onto a clean page. Read all these attributes aloud to yourself. This is you!

As we get to know the attributes of our souls, we need to remember to be kind and encouraging with ourselves. We are learning a new way of relating to the essence of who we are.

2. TAKE STOCK DAILY

The growth of our attributes and our souls is facilitated by taking time each day to reflect on how we are doing. As we retire to bed, for example, we can take a mental note of what we did well and which attributes we used that day. We can also reflect on what situations we could have handled better and which attributes were missing that we could have brought to bear. It is important that in the process of reflecting on our progress, we look at both the positive aspects of our day as well as the areas we would like to improve. We do not grow internally when we take a harsh and unforgiving stance against ourselves. Our inner essence needs gentleness and nurturing encouragement if it is to grow, and there is nothing to be gained by taking an overly negative view of ourselves. After all, compassion is one of the attributes, and compassion toward self is necessary. Our goal when fostering the growth of our souls and the development of our attributes is to ensure each day is an improvement on the one before.

3. ENGAGE WITH LIFE AS AN OPPORTUNITY TO DEVELOP THE ATTRIBUTES

Our attributes grow as we use them when we engage with our families, our co-workers and our communities. We can expect, therefore, that life would present us with opportunities to use and grow our attributes. If we are to develop the attribute of generosity, we can expect to encounter situations where generosity is required. In a similar vein, might we not also expect to face challenges that would make us more patient or more determined? When we start to consider the circumstances of our lives as the lessons and experiences we need to develop our attributes, we resist less and take in the wisdom of each moment however sweet and joyful or hard and painful it might be. To build skills in seeing which attributes we use in our daily lives, we can write down any tasks we carried out or interactions we had recently. We can then list the attributes we used to complete the tasks or facilitate the interactions, thus bringing into our awareness how our daily lives provide opportunities to use and develop our attributes.

4. MEDITATE, PRAY, REFLECT

The practices of prayer and meditation recommended in all spiritual traditions allow us to connect and interact with our souls and our attributes. Prayer feeds our soul in much the same way food nourishes our physical body. Prayer is the practice of asking or supplicating a Higher Power, or praising and expressing gratitude. And just like we converse with one another by speaking and listening, we can think of prayer as the time we speak to that Higher Power, and meditation as the time that we listen for what that Higher Power wants us to know. Our prayer to grow in the attributes and our reflection and meditation on how to do this are a critical part of developing the attributes of our souls.

Recollections: The Lion and the Deer

It is May 19, 2021. I wake up and my face feels tight and pain-ful. I go to the bathroom and the reflection staring back at me is that of an alien: my face and neck are swollen beyond recognition, my eyes are tiny slits and my face is covered with an oozing rash. I feel an equal measure of mental distress and physical discomfort, and I walk to the kitchen to present myself to my husband and daughter. Both attempt to be encouraging, but I can tell from the look in their eyes that they are alarmed. I call my naturopath to see if she has time to see me. She does not, but tells me I can send her a picture of my face. I do this, and she writes back that I should start Prednisone as soon as possible. I laugh to myself: I am in trouble when my naturo-path is recommending a steroid. Over the next weeks, I spend my days in doctors' offices and my nights switching between taking hot baths and cold showers in an effort to get comfort-able. I worry about not knowing the cause of this reaction and I worry about all the work I am not doing. I go through bottles of calamine lotion and I am worn out and scared. Apparently I am having an allergic reaction, but the allergen has not been identified. I notice I am short-tempered and snapping at my family. I am calling out things I do not like, such as the mess in the kitchen, in ways I never have before and my husband jokes that he prefers the old Kadzo. My naturopath tells me that the high histamine levels during an allergic reaction can make me irritable. I ask myself: what is the meaning of this illness?

I pray for healing and pick a card from the Alana Fairchild Rumi Oracle card deck I use for meditation. The card is The Lion and the Deer, and these words jump out at me:

"You are the lion and the deer. You are bold, fierce and vibrant, and you are silent, sweet and gentle. If I should come to you in arrogance you roar at me until my falsehood quakes in fear, so terrified it gives up the game and love's conquest happens yet again! If I should come to you in surrendered adoration, open to whatever you may wish, you are so gentle with me."[1]

I reach out to my dear friend and chiropractor Faraneh Carnegie-Hargreaves hoping for some insight from her deep wisdom. I tell her about my allergic reaction and I share my thoughts on the Rumi card I picked. Faraneh shares that to be authentic in all our relationships, we need to be able to respond to what is in front of us without any preconceived notions of who we are or how we should respond. I feel a light bulb go on in my head. I realize that even as I am struggling with my symptoms, I am growing into "lion." For most of my life I have thought of myself as a quiet, gentle person, but much of how I am supposed to be in the world was prescribed for me. My cultural background only allowed me to be nice and gentle. I was neither allowed to call people out when they were being unjust, nor could I speak my truth. It occurs to me that much of how I was supposed to be was how women survived in the patriarchy of my culture. The physical drama of this allergic reaction has something to teach me. I am learning I need to drop the imposed mythology of having to be a certain way in the world, and become free to respond as called for in any given situation. As the card says:

"*Perhaps what is being unearthed in you now is darker—your sacred rage, refusal to accept disrespect in your life, your inability to tolerate lies and deceptions. Well then, you are the lion, and the deer. That is nature. There is to be both in the world. You are not becoming contradictory or hypocritical. You are becoming whole.*"[2]

I have been comfortable with being gentle most of my life, but have never embraced my fierce side. Although the idea of being the lion is new to me, I can feel the growth toward greater authenticity and a truer way of being in the world. In my office, I hang two framed black-and-white photos I took in Kenya of a lioness showing her teeth and a group of impala grazing to remind myself to embody both the lion and the deer.

CHAPTER 4

Embrace Your Duality

A s if falling into a volcano, I felt myself slipping deeper and deeper into darkness. I was scrolling through social media during a break in my work day, and even as I enjoyed the photos and videos—and resonated deeply with some thought-provoking captions—my mood was changing and feelings of inferiority and inadequacy were beginning to surface. I chastised myself for comparing myself to others, and continued scrolling. My thoughts traveled to an even darker place and I asked myself whether, given all that is already being shared by everyone, I had anything of value to contribute to the world. I was overwhelmed, but I also knew I had work to do, so I took a deep breath, closed the application and prepared for my next client.

I usually pray before I meet my clients, and the prayer I said that day reminded me that through the Creator's power I could offer healing medicine for troubled hearts. The thought that healing did not come from me, but from the Creator working through me, both humbled and strengthened me, and I focused on being a channel for the Creator's grace to the woman I was about to meet. She had been sexually abused by her manager at work and was struggling with symptoms of PTSD. The session went very well, and my client left feeling calm. I was confident that her traumatic memory had been cleared, and I felt elated. My heart expanded with joy as I realized I was doing exactly what I was supposed to do on this planet.

This all-too-familiar swing between my lower self and its feelings of inferiority and self-pity, and my higher self and its humility and compassion is a reality I face every day. I have come to understand that it is part of human nature. Each of us has a lower and higher self, and the inner struggle we feel between these two parts is an inherent aspect of human existence.

The Higher and Lower Self

Societies have long recognized the duality of human existence. In a well-known Cherokee legend, an old man teaches his grandson about life.

> "A fight is going on inside me," he says to the boy. "It is a terrible fight and it is between two wolves. One is evil—he is anger, envy, sorrow, regret, greed, arrogance, self-pity, guilt, resentment, inferiority, lies, false pride, superiority and ego." He continues, "The other is good—he is joy, peace, love, hope, serenity, humility, kindness, benevolence, empathy, generosity, truth, compassion and faith. The same fight is going on inside you—and inside every other person, too." The grandson thinks about it for a minute and then asks his grandfather, "Which wolf will win?" The old Cherokee simply replies, "The one you feed."[1]

This exchange is a profound yet simple conversation which normalizes the inner struggle that is an inherent part of human existence and provides a useful metaphor for understanding some dynamics of spiritual growth. We have already discussed the existence of the intangible part of every human being—the soul. Our souls have needs which are expressed in our search for meaning, purpose and connection; the joy, peace, love and hope which characterize the good wolf are the attributes of our souls. For its life on earth, the soul is associated with the human body, which is a physical entity, so a human being is made up of a physical body and a non-physical soul. If we are to thrive, we must meet our physical needs for food, shelter and protection, and in so doing we can become vulnerable to greed, envy and all the vices that the Cherokee grandfather warns his grandson about.

There are a number of versions of this Cherokee legend, and all of them point to the duality of human nature. We all have souls or a spiritual nature that aspires to goodness, beauty and truth, and a physical nature that, if unchecked, tends toward baser human qualities. We can think of these two aspects of ourselves as the higher self and the lower self. In this chapter we will consider why understanding and accepting both of these facets are critical to our spiritual development and the growth of our souls.

Duality as Opportunity

There is tremendous wisdom and beauty in how the young Cherokee boy is introduced to the dynamic between his spiritual and physical nature. What is particularly powerful in this conversation is that the grandfather grants his grandson control of his own growth and development. In communicating to the boy that he has the power to choose his own path, the grandfather entrusts the boy to take charge of the kind of person he wishes to become and the kind of life he wishes to lead. This choice is open to all of us: we can choose to live acknowledging the spiritual nature of our souls. When we are self-aware, we cannot help but notice the tension between the lower tendencies of our physical nature and the higher tendencies of our spiritual nature. Our spiritual work lies in the choice we make about which part of our nature we develop, or which wolf we feed.

As always, reality is more nuanced than the metaphors we use to understand it. This story portrays the duality of human nature, but we are more complex than is implied in the dichotomy between purely evil and purely good dimensions. For example, while we would agree that anger and greed are negative qualities, when expressed in the interests of increasing justice or fighting inequality, they can become sources of good. Similarly, positive attributes can be a source of evil if not applied with wisdom. For example, truth spoken without tact can cause harm and pain.

We should also note an important aspect of the relationship between our spiritual nature and our physical nature is that the physical is an instrument for the growth of the spiritual while on earth. For example, we demonstrate the spiritual quality of kindness through manifesting the physical act of helping someone or giving what we have. According to many of the world's spiritual traditions, at the end of our human existence the soul leaves the physical body with only the spiritual qualities it has developed.

The duality of human existence and the dynamic between our spiritual and physical natures are what provides us with the opportunity to grow. We experience spiritual victories and the breakthroughs we make, not *in spite of* but *because of* the existence of our lower nature. While we strive to express more and more of our spiritual nature and subdue our lower physical nature, we must consciously embrace our duality. That is how we grow.

Why Hide from a Part of You?

The aspects of their internal dialogue my clients share with me have taught me that too many of us are struggling with the "not so nice" aspects of being human we recognize in ourselves. We struggle with anger, envy, low self-esteem and resentment, and we conclude that having these feelings means there is something wrong with us. This is because as we were growing up we were not given critical information about human nature: every human being has a lower self and a higher self. This is part of our design, and accepting our two natures is an important prerequisite to growing into our full power.

Why are we so uncomfortable with acknowledging our lower nature—the anger, envy, greed, self-pity, arrogance—which exists in all of us? Perhaps one reason is that as children many of us did not have our struggles with anger, disappointment, sorrow or regret validated. Instead, we were met with admonitions to cheer up or reminders that others were much worse off. These well-meaning efforts to move us quickly from feelings of disappointment, sadness or frustration taught us from an early age that those feelings were not acceptable. We learned to be uncomfortable with any manifestation of our lower selves, and to hide aspects of ourselves that were not accepted by those around us. We learned to disapprove of and disconnect from our lower self.

Many of us also grew up in families that celebrated what we did well, and punished us for being stubborn or selfish or angry. As children, we learned that when we were in a good mood or happy we were okay to be around. We were praised when we were kind or friendly. Our tantrums of frustration or anger, on the other hand, were punished with time-outs, angry words or physical violence without clear communication that it was our behavior—and not us—that was unacceptable. Instead of being disciplined for our mistakes and encouraged to do better, we were shamed for any manifestations of the lower self. Sadly, these formative experiences meant that we became comfortable with the manifestation of our higher self, but felt that any of the tendencies of our lower self meant we were fundamentally flawed. As children, many of us learned that to thrive we would need to hide our lower self not just from others, but also from ourselves.

Where has this rejection of the lower self led us? My observation has been that some of our mental distress is caused by harshly judging any of our lower self's tendencies, and concluding that we are terrible and unworthy human beings. Our judgmental thoughts about normal human struggles can also spin off into feelings of depression or anxiety. The ways in which I hear women speak about themselves has taught me that we are harsh and critical of ourselves in ways we would never be if we were talking to anyone else. Our encounters with our lower self lead to unnecessary self-denigration.

The questionable credit of facilitating my own conscious acknowledgment of my lower self goes to my husband. No one prepared me for the fact that I would find in my spouse a mirror constantly reflecting the truth of who I am. There was no hiding from all my moments of stubbornness, self-doubt and resentment with a witness in such close proximity. I remember a time when I was deeply hurt and sobbing about one of my relative's comments, and my husband reminded me to assume that the individual's intentions were pure. I was not ready to hear this and I became angry with him for taking sides. With time I have come to recognize that this kind of defense response that arises in me during interactions with my husband is sometimes an indicator I need to face a difficult truth about myself. I also learned the moments I flinch about what is going on inside me are the ones in which I need to pay extra attention. In these moments, an aspect of my lower self is coming to the surface and I am being presented with an opportunity to grow spiritually by being more forgiving or more compassionate. The acceptance of the lower self clearly shows us the path toward where we specifically need to grow. We can subdue our vulnerabilities by knowing and accepting them, and as we humbly accept our own struggles we also become more compassionate about the struggles of those around us.

Some of the clients I see identify with their lower nature and cannot see or accept their higher nature. Women in particular seem vulnerable to identifying with their negative tendencies and losing sight of their positive qualities. This was, and maybe still is, true of me too. Ironically, the same mirror I found in my husband that showed me my dark side with agonizing accuracy has also been the mirror that introduced me to the possibility that I have a higher self. I grew up in a culture where feedback on what I needed to change and what I was doing wrong came at me fast and furiously. Positive reinforcement, not so much. I vividly remember sitting in my college room in my early twenties and reading Marianne Williamson's words with great puzzlement, "Our deepest fear is that we are powerful beyond measure. It is our light, not our darkness that most frightens us."[2] How is it even possible that I have any light within me? It seemed like a wonderful idea and something I wanted to believe, but I really did not understand it. It has been the consistent love and affirmation over twenty-five years from my husband, the same man who reflects when I am coming from my lower self, that has helped bring me to a place where I can sit comfortably with my higher self. In my case, the mirror that invited me to a more accurate view of myself came primarily from my husband, but mirrors are to be found in many of the relationships we have where we know our perfectly imperfect selves are honored and loved.

The acceptance of the higher self puts us in touch with the gifts we bring to the world and the potential we have to contribute to society in meaningful ways. Let us not hide from any part of ourselves, but instead accept both the lower and higher self as who we are. We are here to grow, subdue the lower self and contribute to the world from the noble soul within us.

The Power of Advance Notice

What if, from an early age, we received some form of the wise counsel of the Cherokee grandfather? What if we had been introduced as young children to the idea that human beings have a higher and a lower nature, and that these parts of ourselves grow to the extent that we nurture them? We would certainly have more compassion for our weaknesses. We would also be more likely to acknowledge and accept our challenges with less judgment and more understanding, because we would be aware that everyone has some level of inner struggle between their higher and lower selves.

If we knew from the outset that it is natural to have noble tendencies toward attributes like love and courage, as well as baser tendencies toward arrogance, greed and self-pity, we would allow ourselves honest personal inventories of our inner state. We would be more comfortable with the kind of truthful self-evaluation that is a prerequisite to spiritual growth. Most importantly, we would be equipped with a worldview that would allow us true acceptance of our inner being's current state, even as we continue to strive for growth and prosperity.

Understanding that our souls grow as a result of the interplay between our higher and lower selves also allows us to take a dynamic view of our spiritual growth. We let go of the idea that we are either good or bad, and instead take on the more accurate perspective that we are creatures in a constant state of flux. Sometimes we make great strides forward and win inner victories quickly, sometimes our growth is slow and sometimes we take steps backward. We allow ourselves grace and forgive ourselves when we make mistakes. I once heard a young woman apologize to a friend she had been impatient with with the words, "I am so sorry, my higher self went on a mini-vacation and my lower self took over. Please forgive me." I was very impressed by this exchange, and have sought to follow this young woman's example. The ability to observe our own behavior, take responsibility for it and frame it in the context of the battle between the higher and lower self is within reach for all of us. If we learn how to navigate the battle between our higher and lower selves—and we teach this to all those whose lives we touch—we will all be stronger human beings. At its simplest level, this might look like recognizing the options we have in how we respond when someone upsets us. Our lower self might be tempted to attack or hurt the individual, and our higher self might be inclined to clearly communicate what happened to us and what we would have preferred to see happen. Becoming comfortable with both our lower and higher self supports us in attaining the inner peace that comes with knowing and accepting who we are, including our victories and our struggles.

Acknowledging the dynamics of growth and the struggle between the higher and lower self also allows us to be more compassionate with ourselves and others. Seeing ourselves as having choices about which side we wish to manifest gives us room for much more self-compassion and less judgment regarding our struggles. We move away from thinking in terms of the existence of good and bad people to living in a world where people have the capacity for both bad and good. We can take an open and humble stance toward others and ourselves.

The Value of Contrast

My clients are often mystified by their ability to both do kind things and to do cruel things. This duality is disconcerting to them, and yet it is important for their mental health that this dilemma is resolved. The power inherent in accepting the dual nature of human beings is beautifully illustrated in the work of Dr. Jennifer Gaudiani who describes in her book *Sick Enough* how she uses the metaphor of a two-sided coin to teach her clients about the relationships between their strengths and their darker side. She writes, "While my patients get lots of attention for the golden side of their coin, they often don't get support for their darker side. In part they've worked hard to look like they don't have a darker side."[3] The goal, Dr. Gaudiani continues, "is to help remind them that they are allowed to be both sides of their coin and to honor both."[3]

As we have evolved as a species, we have had different narratives to explain the inner struggle between the higher and lower selves. Some of these narratives externalize the source of our baser tendencies to outside forces, and rob us of the power inherent in taking responsibility for the things we do that are less than noble. When we externalize the source of our lower tendencies, we also deprive ourselves of understanding the value and power of our higher nature. For example, as we take stock of how our day went, we might notice that when someone took the parking spot we had been waiting for we did not swear at them as we might have done in the past. Instead, we took deep breaths and went to find another spot. We can only fully appreciate the value and power of our higher nature if we also acknowledge our lower nature. What power is there in manifesting generosity when the tendency to be selfish has nothing to do with us? We manifest our true power to be generous in the face of the option to be selfish. The victory of being our best selves is made sweeter by the existence of a very different alternative, not because there is no alternative. What is the value of spiritual growth if there is no contrast to it? We would not know the power of the higher nature were it not for the contrast we see with our lower nature. Therefore, as we mature as women, let us recognize that the potential to both do what is honorable and what is abasing lies in each of us. As we saw in the Cherokee tale, we have the power to choose whether we nurture the higher self or the lower self. Our higher nature has the capacity to subdue our lower nature, and subduing our lower selves is the process of spiritual growth.

If the notion of having a lower self is disconcerting, it may help to recognize that this is an integral part of the human condition. When we meet someone who seems consistently kind and consistently trustworthy, we should see them as a victor of their inner battles, and also recognize that they have their own struggles with their lower nature. Accepting the duality of our inner nature brings with it peace of mind that we are not alone in our daily striving to do better.

Be the Rider and the Horse

Sigmund Freud, the founder of psychoanalysis, used the metaphor of a rider and a horse to portray the struggle between two aspects of his understanding of human personality. He called the wild and impulsive part of us the id and the more rational, logical part the super-ego.[4] The metaphor of the horse and the rider has also been used in psychology to illustrate the ways different parts of the brain function, and the struggle between the logical brain and the emotional brain.[5] It has also been suggested that we can choose whether we are the horse or the rider. However, when it comes to fostering our spiritual growth, it is more helpful to think of ourselves as both. We can consider our higher self as the rider and the lower self as a wild horse that can be trained by a skillful rider. As we develop the capacities of the higher self and subdue the capacities of the lower self, we gain an increasing ability to control the tendencies of our lower self and manifest the capacities of our higher self. Just as the rider gains mastery over the wild horse with skillful training, our higher self gains mastery over the lower self through patient and diligent striving.

When we understand these dynamics of growth for ourselves, we open the door to all those who will follow us and whose lives we touch. Our friends, our partners, our siblings, our children and even our parents will benefit when we move into the position of being both the masterful, highly skilled rider and also being the wild horse. As we learn to subdue the lower self, we can stand in our true power.

As my own journey of striving to manifest my higher self and subdue my lower self continues, I notice I am better able to remain centered as I scroll through social media, but I am a work in progress.

With our understanding of the duality of human nature, and our awareness of the attributes of the soul, let us now consider the idea of purpose in life and how it relates to our spiritual growth in the next chapter.

TO GO DEEPER

*The Journey toward Manifesting
the Higher Self*

Here are some guideposts for the journey of nurturing
the higher self and gaining mastery over the lower self.

1. START WITH TAKING INVENTORY

Embarking on a journey to develop the higher self
and subdue the lower self begins by taking inventory
of where we are. The intention is to compassionately
and lovingly look at ourselves honestly so we can
determine the steps we want to take to grow. A simple
way to do this is to use a notebook. Reflect on and
write down times you have been aware of coming
from your higher nature, and what that felt like. Also
reflect on and write down when you have come from
your lower nature and what emotions that brought
up for you. Next, for each of the ways you manifested
your higher and your lower self, ask yourself with
loving curiosity how you learned to behave in that
way. As we consciously observe our higher nature
and our lower nature, and recognize the dilemmas
and struggles we face as these two parts of our reality
interact, we strengthen our power to make changes.

2. CONSCIOUSLY FOSTER YOUR GROWTH

As spiritual beings we are always in a state of change,
either growing or regressing. With the passage of

time many of us develop insight and grow without striving to do so, but there is often unnecessary suffering that accompanies growth when we are not in the driver's seat of our lives. The conscious fostering of our growth puts us in control of our soul's growth. This can be done by consciously setting the intention each morning to change one aspect about the way you have typically handled a situation from the lower self, and manifesting your higher self in the same situation. For example, if you have impatiently raised your voice at family members during your morning routine, plan not to raise your voice and instead show more patience. This kind of conscious fostering of our own growth in different areas of our lives puts us in the arena of self-mastery and personal power.

3. REFLECT

The conscious reflection of how we are doing in manifesting our higher self is a key factor in fostering the development of our souls. There will be times when insights will drop in like pleasant surprises as we become aware of a victory in how we chose to act or not act in a particular situation. There will also be times when that awareness unfolds gradually if we stay committed to developing our souls. Our reflection or mental inventory at the end of the day is also the means by which we can reflect on how well we are nurturing the growth of the higher self, and how much control we have over the tendencies of our lower self.

4. BE PATIENT

Spiritual growth and the development of our souls takes time: it is actually our life's purpose. If you are on the planet, there is some growing and learning to do. Modern Western culture has become one of quick results and instant communication, so it is important to note the growth of the soul is a process that takes time. Be patient with yourself and hold the same compassion for your own growth that you would hold for a toddler learning to walk.

5. BE OUTWARD LOOKING

The process of growth is not dissimilar to watching a rose bloom. If you sit still and watch the rose continuously, you can become impatient. However, if you walk away for a while and come back, you see how much the rose has opened. If, rather than focusing constantly on our internal landscape, we were to "look away" by engaging in something that supports others or makes the earth a better place, we would notice the changes in ourselves that take place when our focus is elsewhere. We would also likely find the changes we notice might not have occurred had we remained focused on our internal dynamics. Our higher self grows most when it is looking outward and serving the needs of others. A good way to start might be to find volunteer opportunities in your community that take your attention away from your own needs.

Recollections: Drifting?

"You are making the biggest mistake of your life! What are you doing?" I am on a phone call listening to a colleague in wildlife conservation share her strong views about my decision to quit my job and go to the United States with the man who will soon become my husband. I am surprised she knows the news I shared with my officemates just three days ago. I am not used to people paying attention to the events of my life, but it seems that—at least this once—my life is newsworthy.

"Talking to strangers about our problems, that's not something we do!" I hear my father say these words and I know that becoming a psychologist is not an option. My parents have strong views about what is a respectable course of study at university. I know sciences are on the short menu of options, so I randomly pick one. Some months later, I am on a plane heading to England to study zoology at the University of Oxford.

The laboratory is cold and brightly lit, and I am looking carefully at an octopus and making a drawing of it. I look to my right and notice that my friend's drawing, with all its detailed intricacy, looks like a diagram in a textbook. I realize I am in a class with people who have been picking up and studying

worms, frogs and other critters since they were three. I wonder if studying zoology is a mistake, but my family has invested so much money in my education that I brush off the thought and continue with my drawing.

My attention is captivated by a conservation biology professor who is lecturing animatedly about the dangers to butterfly populations and what can be done to save them. I am finally hearing something I can get excited about, and I sense that my desire to make a difference in the world may find expression in conservation.

As I walk past the faculty offices in the zoology department, one of my professors sees me through the glass walls and beckons me to come in. My professor has a visitor and he introduces me, "Kadzo, meet Iain Douglas-Hamilton. He is from Kenya and he is an expert on elephants." My professor turns to Iain and says, "Iain, find something for Kadzo to do this summer when she comes home." Iain and I speak for a few moments and he gives me his card saying, "Call me when you get home."

Some weeks pass and I am seated at an outdoor restaurant in Nairobi under the shade of a tall tree with bright orange blooms. I am having lunch with Iain Douglas-Hamilton. A lady happens to walk by our table, sees Iain and stops to say hello. Iain introduces me to Cynthia Moss, the director of the Amboseli Elephant Project. Iain asks Cynthia if she needs a student on the project. Cynthia says yes, and takes my number. Two weeks later I am in a large vehicle going to a national park in Kenya for the first time. At the end of that summer I have funding to do a Ph.D. on the Amboseli elephants.

I am sitting on the bleachers at my daughter's high school, watching her play field hockey as one of a strong line of defenders. I smile as I realize the defiant fierceness she manifested as a four-year-old is exactly the strength she now needs on the field. I enjoy the warm sunlight on my skin and the opportunity to visit with the other parents, and I am grateful that we organize our lives so I can be there to see my daughter play.

Looking back, it seems I drifted from one opportunity that presented itself to the next without really thinking about what I wanted to do with my life. Reflecting on this pattern, I remembered a conversation between my parents in which they were discussing a suitable career path for me without asking me any questions. It was as if I was not in the room. Maybe this is one of the reasons I learned not to take full agency over my life. I believe the first truly proactive decisions I made came in my late twenties when I chose to get married and when I chose to stay home to raise my children. I also chose to do some career testing in my thirties that led me into mental health. Perhaps being open to the opportunities that came my way in the early stages of my life was the path I had to take to get to where I needed to be.

What I think of as my three careers—wildlife conservation, motherhood and psychotherapy—were and are all driven by the desire to make the world better. Looking back, I feel I have learned that true purpose is found in the motive to contribute to society, and that purpose is less about what we do and more about what motivates us to do it.

CHAPTER 5

Know Your Purpose

In my work with trauma, I sometimes see several members of a family who experienced the same traumatic event. This was the case with my client Marcy, whom I saw for three sessions to address the impact of a car accident. Some weeks after Marcy's treatment ended, her mother Erin asked if she could see me to address the symptoms she had been experiencing since the accident. In addition to focusing on the trauma from the car accident, Erin also wanted to discuss her struggle with feeling she was not accomplished enough.

"I feel I have wasted my life, and I have nothing to show for myself even though I turn fifty in a couple of years."

"It's interesting you say that," I responded. "I get the sense that you love Marcy dearly, don't you?"

"Oh yes, I do. Both she and her brother are really cool kids."

I decided to use humor and exaggeration to bring Erin's attention to the fact that she was discounting the time she had spent raising her children, so I teased her about her life choices with some drama.

"So, raising two wonderful children is worth nothing and you have nothing to show for your life? I know your daughter is thoughtful, insightful and kind. I have not met your son, but from what you are saying both of them are amazing."

"Okay, if you put it like that . . . " Erin said as she started laughing.

Like Erin, many women discount the value of the time and effort they take to raise their children, but we know if mothers stopped doing what they do all of humanity would come to a standstill. What if we created a society which supported women like Erin to feel like they are fulfilling an invaluable role and important purpose by raising their children?

Rethinking Purpose

We often speak of the need to find our purpose, so let us be clear about what we mean. One dictionary definition of purpose is, "The reason something is done or created or for which something exists."[1] This implies that if we have purpose or there is a reason we are here, that purpose originates from something other than ourselves—or at least exists outside ourselves. If we are here for a reason, or if there is something particular for us to do while on this planet, then the reason for our existence would not originate from us. However, we speak and behave as if it is up to us to define our purpose and manifest it, and therein lies part of the quandary of being human. We like the idea that there might be something for us to accomplish with our unique array of gifts and talents, but few of us consider the actual source of human purpose, and some of us are uncomfortable with the idea that a sense of purpose might come from outside ourselves. We want to have a mission in life with no reference to a mission control center. But the notion of purpose does not make sense without some reference to the idea of a grand design of which we are a part: something outside ourselves that infuses us with a sense of what we are here to accomplish. Of course, it is entirely up to each of us to consider the source of our purpose, or what it is that confers us with a sense of purpose. For some it will be God and for others the Universe, but purpose must be related to something greater than ourselves whether or not we choose to acknowledge it.

The term "purpose" has also become closely related with the work we do to earn our livelihoods. We can hardly be blamed for this: our materialistic society, with its tendency to monetize everything, has also monetized our understanding of purpose. So much of the media we consume encourages us to think about purpose in a way that makes it about what we do for financial gain. This commoditizing and reduction of our sense of purpose to the work we do for a living not only keeps us in the rat race to do more, achieve more and earn more, but also disconnects us from the core of who we are. As the meaning of purpose and work have merged, purpose has become all about performing, producing and doing. Dr. Brené Brown, research professor and author, states that while we live in a society that highly values work, "in many cases the meaningful work is not what pays the bills"[2] and encompasses the many dimensions of our lives like parenting, volunteering and hobbies. This full expression of our gifts and talents in the world, beyond how we earn our livelihoods, is the expression of our noble souls that will lead us to the sense of fulfillment we are seeking. We manifest our gifts more fully when we consider purpose an expression of our souls. In this chapter we will explore the idea of purpose as it relates to the core of who we are and our innate blueprint as noble souls.

Purpose and Design

We know a car is manufactured to transport us from one point to another, and everything about it is designed to accomplish its purpose. The idea that purpose and design are linked can be helpful in considering our own purpose. My clients' questions about purpose typically emerge after their disturbing symptoms have subsided, and are usually some variation of, "Now that I am better, what do I do with my life?" Or simply, "What is my purpose?" I usually respond by asking their questions back at them, and I am often met with puzzled looks and shrugs. However, given a little room, my clients' inherent sense of purpose comes bubbling to the surface. Over years of asking my clients to simply fill in the blank in the phrase, "A chair is to sit on, a knife is to cut, a human is to ____, "[3] the answers they have come up with are always some form of love, help, care or serve. It seems we have an intuitive sense that our purpose as human beings includes relating to others in a way that supports them.

It is not a revolutionary concept that we are here to serve others. We all speak of the value of service. What we might need to add to our understanding is the idea that service is an expression of our souls. Service is not just something we do because it feels good. We feel good when we are of service to others because in serving we are aligning with what we are designed to do. Human beings are designed to serve others, and all our human faculties and capacities are exactly as they need to be for us to fulfill this purpose. We are living to true purpose and intended design when we serve, and we feel good when we are fulfilling our purpose.

Once we understand that we are here to serve, we can reframe our ideas about what it looks like to be living our true purpose. What we do as paid work can be service, but so is everything else we do selflessly to support those around us. In fact, most of what we do in service to others is not paid work. We serve our families, our friends and our communities in large and small ways all the time. Cooking dinner, helping a toddler put on their clothes and doing yard work for an elderly neighbor are all acts of service.

We saw in Chapter 3 that our souls are endowed with attributes we are here to develop, and we have spoken of our spiritual growth as the process of growing our attributes. Logically, therefore, another element of human purpose is to develop our spiritual attributes and to become more loving, just, patient and generous. When we consider these attributes in the context of purpose, we see that in meeting the purpose of being of service to others we automatically develop our attributes. The development of the attributes of our souls and service to others are inextricably linked: we cannot grow our attributes in isolation, and it is when we engage and serve one another that our attributes develop and we grow spiritually.

Taken together, these two elements of purpose—serving others and growing spiritually by developing our attributes— help us understand that we can stay true to purpose even when the details of what we are doing changes over time.

What about Our Unique Expression of Purpose?

So far we have discussed how being of service and growing spiritually by developing the attributes of our souls are purposes we all share. How do we find our particular way of expressing this two-fold purpose? How do we discover how we can serve with the unique endowment of gifts and talents we have?

Each individual's particular calling lies somewhere in our answer to what troubles us most about the world we live in, and what brings us joy. What in the news really upsets you? That might be a clue to what you are most passionate about. Magic happens when we combine this passion with our sense of what brings us joy and feels effortless. Some of us are furious that we continue to use the earth's resources irresponsibly, so we act in ways to protect the environment. Others are motivated to address gender inequality and dedicate their lives to bring about social justice. Sometimes we can find our unique expression of purpose by considering what we would be happy to do without compensation.

Discovering how we are meant to manifest our unique gifts and talents also involves a deep inner dialogue with our souls. We need to approach our lives in a posture of learning and open ourselves to receiving guidance that will either confirm that we are on the right path or that we need to make some adjustments. Acting and then reflecting on the outcome is a powerful path to manifesting purpose, as illustrated in a conversation I had with a friend as we sat at an outdoor cafe a few summers ago.

"I wonder when to stop pushing. You know how we think we have to work hard and keep trying and never give up? But this project I've been working on just does not seem to be going anywhere."

In our conversation that day, we explored the idea that when a project does not progress, this might be guidance from the Universe to place our efforts elsewhere. We discussed how counter-cultural it can seem not to keep pursuing the goals we set for ourselves, and also how some things we pursue seem effortless. We concluded that we would both become more open to signals on how to proceed and to think of doors closing as an opportunity to reevaluate, and of doors opening as a sign we are on the right track.

Perhaps our tendency to push hard to accomplish things is a dynamic we have inherited from the patriarchal way of being in the world. What if things can actually move more smoothly if we really tune in to the signs we receive about the direction we should be taking?

Motherhood as Purpose

As we have seen, when we confuse our purpose with what we do for a living, we are blind to the fact that much of what we do that is not compensated financially is also part of our purpose. Like my client Erin, we are vulnerable to thinking we have no purpose. However, the roles we play as mothers, mentors, spouses, daughters, friends and caregivers are critical to society. The contribution women make by nurturing others is currently the most undervalued service to humanity, yet one of the most important for its progress. I focus on mothers in this section because this is a book for women, but of course fathers also have critical roles to play in raising children and should also be supported.

Can we imagine a world in which mothers everywhere are valued, empowered to raise their children and appreciated for fulfilling this important role in society? What if we acknowledged the time and effort it takes to raise children who can foster unity with people of different backgrounds, care for the planet and value themselves as noble beings? In one generation, change could be accomplished the likes of which we have yet to witness. A global effort to ensure the conscious, deliberate, kind and thorough attention to raising children would profoundly change humanity's fortunes. If we appreciated what mothers contribute to society, we would create policies which support parents caring for their offspring, we would create community networks to support mothers and their children, and mothers would be accorded the respect they deserve.

This does not mean women would not have broader roles in society at large, but rather we would rethink the way society supports mothers during the early years of their children's lives. These years are when critical brain development takes place and the habits of thought and action that shape a child's character are being developed. When we think of the direction we want the world to take, we must recognize that motherhood is a high-level purpose. Mothering involves holding a space for the development and manifestation of another soul's full potential, as well as letting it know it is fully seen and will continue to be fully seen until it can see itself fully. Mothering is a spiritual purpose.

Of course women are not limited to nurturing roles. Women today lead countries and governments, they are scientists, engineers, construction workers, nurses and doctors. They participate in all spheres of life, and create a world of possibility for all women and generations to come.

My experience of having babies and toddlers was exhausting, confusing and even harrowing at times. I went from being an expert whose opinion on human-elephant conflict was sought out, to being passed over at parties by people more interested in talking to my husband, the professional. As life would have it, even as I struggled with motherhood, I needed to revisit my commitment to staying home to raise my children more than once. When my son was five and my daughter was three, I was offered my dream job in conservation. I made the decision to continue to stay home with my children based on this thought, "When I lie down in bed at 50, what will I regret more: not spending time with my children, or not having a great career in conservation?" It was an easy decision to make, but it was also a very difficult decision to live with. I no longer had the work credentials the world valued. I felt worthless in a society that has not learned to value and acknowledge mothers. I remember calling my husband at his place of work in tears knowing he could do little to help me, but needing to reach out to another adult and share the feeling of loneliness and isolation that plagued me each day.

Mothering young children was a challenging existence. My days were filled with trips to libraries and playgrounds, craft projects and messy baking sessions. I did my best to be upbeat and cheerful around my children, and I was very grateful that I was able to be with them. However, I also missed the validation I received when I worked outside the home. My husband would hold me when I cried at night about how disempowered I felt, and he did everything he could to make my life easier when he was home.

Fifty is now in the rearview mirror for me, and I have no regrets about staying home to raise my children. In fact, I look back and I am beyond thankful that I could take that time. I realize that stepping off the career track helped me pivot my life in a way that may never have happened otherwise. I feel grateful for the deep trust there is between me and my children, and I know it is the result of the years we spent together. If there is something I could change about my time mothering children, I would go back and be happier. I did what I needed to do, but if I had known where that was leading me, I would have delighted in each day. Of course I could not have foreseen exactly the direction my life would take, but if I had believed early on that life unfolds as it needs to, perhaps I might have been happier on the journey.

The challenge of valuing motherhood as purpose was a journey of growth for me. Without knowing at the time, choosing to stay at home to raise my children was one of the best decisions I have made. It taught me something I have come to hold true about how life unfolds: when we make decisions with good intentions, the universe rewards us. Motherhood certainly tore me apart while I was in the trenches—the constant diaper changes, the sleepless nights, the meal preparation and the relentless toddler questions were exhausting. However, the pieces of me came back together in a more beautiful way than I could have imagined. My patience and capacity to love grew so much and I tapped into deeper wisdom as I dedicated myself as best I could to educating and training the next generation. If one of the purposes of life is to grow spiritually, then motherhood is the fast track!

I recognize choosing to raise my children was a privilege many do not have and staying home with young children is not financially viable for everyone. But anyone who saw the beat-up car we drove for years knows my family also made some choices about lifestyle that made my staying at home possible. I am also not saying the way I chose to navigate motherhood is how anyone else should do it. I made the choice after reading about the importance of the early years in a child's development, alongside prayerful reflection about what was best for me and my family. Everyone has to make choices based on their circumstances, and there is no one right way of raising children or having a family. Regardless of the choices we make about our work and family life, we know that mothers are critical in shaping the environments within which their children are raised. For me, the investment of time and attention to my children in the early years was a priority which was worth it in the end. I became a wildlife conservationist to change the world, and raising my two children—who had many wild moments of their own—gave me the opportunity to shape the beliefs, faith, thinking and behavior of two human beings, and subsequently those of future generations.

In highlighting the importance of mothers, I intend to bring attention to an area society has fallen way short of in what is needed to ensure humankind's prosperity. I do not wish to detract from the important roles of women who choose not to be mothers or who cannot have children. Future generations benefit from the nurturing and education they receive from many individuals including grandmothers, interested members of their extended families, teachers, coaches and health care workers. I believe the task before us as a society is to begin to ask ourselves what a society that fully supports raising and training the next generation looks like. What policy changes do we need to make? How do we need to adjust our understanding of work to accommodate the unfolding of full potential in our children and young people? How do we build connected communities and neighborhoods that nurture us all?

As we consider our individual purpose, let us regard it in the context of a larger divine purpose, and define purpose more broadly that what we do to earn our livelihood. A broader understanding of purpose might have meant Erin did not feel she had wasted her life by raising her children. In the next chapter we will explore how to foster authentic relationships which are informed by our spiritual reality as souls.

TO GO DEEPER

Dropping into Purpose

The resources for living with deep purpose are already in us. Here are a few pointers for your journey toward connecting with purpose.

1. REFLECT ON WHAT PROBLEM YOU ARE HERE TO SOLVE

What in particular makes you angry or upset about the state of the world? Your passion about a particular issue can be an indicator that you are here to do something about it. What piece of the problem can you see yourself contributing to solve? Write down a few of the problems or crises humanity is facing that catch your interest. Identify which of these you feel strongly about. Next, note down what actions you can take to address it, and what steps you can take toward growing your interest and working toward solving the problem. While some challenges seem far-reaching, efforts at the local level, however small, do make a difference.

2. TAP INTO JOY

Notice what brings you joy. Also notice what you dread. Consider what these feelings are trying to tell you with compassionate curiosity. Make a list of things you are doing currently or have done in the past that have brought you great joy. What can you bring into your life that would add joy to your days? For example, if music or art brings you joy, how can these be built into your life in a way that serves you and others?

3. TUNE INTO THE SIGNS YOU ARE RECEIVING ABOUT THE PATH YOU ARE ON

When things seem to be working effortlessly or without struggle, and doors seem to be opening to you easily, take time to reflect and meditate about what you are experiencing. Become conscious of the forces in the Universe that are supporting you. When you seem to be pushing against an immovable mountain, have the grace to stop and reflect on what messages the Universe is sending you. Prayer and meditation will support you in deciding what your next actions should be. Remember that timing is also critical—a door that remains tightly shut to you at one time could open later. Let go of the need to struggle.

4. MAINTAIN AN OUTWARD-LOOKING LENS

Notice the needs of people around you. Start to serve those needs in small ways, but do not draw attention to the fact you are looking to see what is needed of you. What do you learn about yourself when you serve others without seeking recognition? If you choose to, you can increase the scope of your service. What does your neighborhood need? What does your community need?

Recollections: Prejudice

My family is sitting outside enjoying the warm Nairobi sunshine when we hear a car come up the driveway: my uncle has come to visit. My brother, sister and I all run to greet him. He distributes lollipops after he imparts words of wisdom to each of us individually. When it is my turn, he hands me one green and one purple lollipop. He asks me how I am doing in school and, beaming with pride, I tell him my grades are very good. He tells me I can never marry someone from a certain tribe. I have heard this many times before, and I nod as I put a sticky, tart, lime-flavored lollipop into my mouth.

It is the day before my cousin's wedding, and the women in my family have gathered to prepare food. There are several enormous pots of rice and rich curries cooking on stout charcoal stoves. The air is filled with the fragrance of cardamom and cumin. As teenagers, my cousins and I are expected to help with the cooking, so we sit on a straw mat peeling garlic. The women are talking about the wedding, gossiping and laughing, and the topic of who we should marry comes up. It is the usual reminder not to marry people from the tribe my uncle was talking about.

These days, I am horrified to think how I went along with this system of tribalism. I would meet members of this tribe at school and in my social circles as an adult, and as much as I liked them as individuals, I knew it ended there. These were not the friends to bring home, and definitely not boyfriend material! I share these recollections to highlight the importance of questioning what you are taught about groups of people. I was the product of a very effective mechanism for instilling prejudice, and it was not until my late twenties when I learned about the concept of the oneness of humankind. This woke me up to the notion that the elders I respected and loved could have been wrong in their tribalism and prejudice.

It has been such a wonderful day and my jaw hurts from smiling. I love my cream, silk wedding dress and, at twenty-nine, I feel like a princess holding the hand of my handsome new husband. The ceremony is over and more than 200 of us are seated at tables covered in beautiful white linens and white roses. One of the uncles is giving a speech and he praises us for choosing to get married, "This is the coming together of two races and two families." I turn to look at my husband just as he is turning to look at me. Our eyes meet and we laugh as we realize we are thinking the same thing. We whisper to each other that we had not thought about the other as coming from a different race. We go back to listening to the speech and the festivities continue. My husband is Iranian American and I am Kenyan. I grew up in a society that is so focused on tribe that race was not a consideration in my relationship with him.

My husband, son, daughter and I are sitting at the kitchen counter of our home in Connecticut. My husband is telling our late-teen children how to respond when they are driving and are stopped by the police. I realize that the strategies

my husband is sharing seem logical and work for him, but that our children will have a different experience because of racism. I remind them that there seem to be no rules to avoid police brutality, and that when they are stopped they need to say the prayers we have taught them. I tell them to pray that any officer they meet is one who serves our community with integrity. I notice that in our family there is no trace of the excitement parents should feel when their children get their driving licenses. My heart aches for all the mothers who have lost their children.

CHAPTER 6

Build Authentic Relationships

As a client, Nobuko intrigued me. In her first few sessions it became apparent her value system had contributed to the development of an eating disorder. I felt one of the goals of therapy would be to encourage her to look objectively at her worldview and consider alternatives that could lead to wellness. In one of her sessions she expressed frustration with her habit of comparing herself to other people.

"So, let's take a look at what is going on from a different perspective, because that might give us insight into what you are finding so frustrating," I said, hoping she would accept this invitation to explore.

"Sure," she said, smiling in a way that told me she was thinking she had nothing to lose.

I took a pad of art paper from the shelf next to me and drew a line down the middle with a green pencil. At the top of one side I wrote, "Values" and on the other side I wrote, "How I learned them." I asked Nobuko to tell me what she considered her core values were and how she learned them. I wrote as she spoke, and soon we had captured the following:

- Work hard and do your best—learned from family.

- The golden rule: do unto others as you would like them to do unto you—learned from family.

- People's appearances are an indicator of how much they value health and fitness—learned from social media.

- People's value is related to their appearance—learned from social media.

- People do good things so that they feel good—learned from religious schools.

- Humans are not different from animals—learned from science.

- People are inherently self-interested—learned from what motivates the people I know: my friends want to be doctors because they want to make their mark on the world and also make money.

Based on what Nobuko was telling me, I had a good sense of the direction the session needed to take. I used an analogy I learned from Dr. Jon Connelly.

"Have you ever had an article of clothing you loved so much that you wore it as often as you could, then you started to notice it was becoming threadbare? You saw a small hole, then another and then someone close to you told you it's time to stop wearing it?" I asked.

"Yes, I have a pair of shoes like that."

"Okay. At some point you recognized it was time for a new pair of shoes."

"Yes."

"Well, the same applies to the way we understand the world. When we recognize that our way of seeing things doesn't serve us anymore, we can try a different way of looking at things and experiment with how the new lens might work for us."

Nobuko and I went on to discuss how having an eating disorder was a reasonable life strategy within the framework of her current worldview in which a person's value is related to their appearance. I gently challenged her to consider changing her worldview about what gives people value, and she was open to the idea and promised to journal about it. Nobuko made steady progress in her recovery. Her willingness to consider a more accurate view of herself and the world around her is at the heart of authenticity, which involves the recognition of your own intrinsic value as a noble soul and the intrinsic value and nobility of others. In this chapter we will explore the foundational principles of establishing authentic relationships. We will also look at the barriers within ourselves that prevent us from relating authentically to others. Rather than discussing any particular type of relationship, we will be looking at principles of authenticity that apply to all relationships.

What Is Authenticity and What Are Authentic Relationships?

The word "authentic" implies having a sense of what is real or true. A prerequisite for being in an authentic relationship with others is seeing people as they truly are, with the same noble nature and attributes that we are aware of in ourselves. Professor William Hatcher, mathematician and author of *Love, Power and Justice: The Dynamics of Authentic Morality* states, "We can say that our relationship with any given category of existence is authentic to the degree that it is based on an accurate perception of the structure of reality."[1] To be authentic would mean recognizing the true value of an entity and responding according to this value. Collaborating with Dr. Hatcher and The Authenticity Project, psychotherapist Mary K. Radpour writes:

> "Relationships characterized by *authenticity* are mutually satisfying. Both parties 'win,' since it is profoundly satisfying both to be valued and to offer true affirmation to one another. In fact, this feeling of being recognized for our intrinsic value is the same as the experience of genuine love. *Authenticity* provides the opportunity for truthful sharing, and reciprocity ensures that we both benefit from the sharing."[2]

Radpour goes on to say that authentic relationships encompass all the desires we hold in our hearts for relationships: mutuality, reciprocity, truthfulness, trustworthiness and genuine love.[3] At the heart of our ability to build authentic relationships is our capacity to recognize in others the same values we see in ourselves as noble souls, and to treat them accordingly. Having learned to see our own essence as the repository of wonderful attributes, we extend this view to those around us. A new vista in our relationships opens to us when we are seeking how to serve the nobility in the person we are relating to: we ask ourselves what is needed for that particular soul at that particular moment to affirm their nobility.

Becoming Authentic Women

As women living in a patriarchal society, many of us have forgotten the power we hold, and this manifests in specific ways in our relationships. We forget we have control of who we allow into our inner circle of intimacy, we struggle to remain in spaces where we are not seen, we gravitate toward people who meet our needs in unhealthy ways, and we develop a scarcity mindset that keeps us seeking approval. Taking back control in these four areas is an important first step toward becoming more authentic, so let us look at each one in turn.

Take Control of Who Is in Your Inner Circle

Many of my clients struggle with navigating their social lives. From middle school through college and beyond, there is often a high level of drama in women's social circles, and we often feel that we are victims of these dynamics. An intervention I use to address this is one I learned from Radpour. It involves drawing a number of concentric circles on a blank page with a small x at the center of all the circles. My client Yumi particularly liked this way of thinking.

"So this X is you in the center of all these circles, and each of these circles represents your level of closeness or intimacy with people. The individuals you are closest to, which can be your family or friends, are in the inner circle. The next circle is for friends and family members who are less close to you, until all the way here in the outermost circle are perhaps the people you recognize in passing, but have never spoken to. So my first question to you, Yumi, is who gets to decide where individuals fall in these circles?"

"What do you mean?" she asked.

"Well, who decides if someone is a close friend in this circle here, or way out here?" I pointed to the circles.

"Me?" Yumi asked tentatively.

"Exactly. You get to make that call, and you can decide if someone out here can come in closer and if someone close needs to be further away."

"Oh, I really like that!" Yumi replied.

Yumi went on to experiment with putting herself in the driver's seat of her social life, and the level of drama in her life diminished. As women, we would do well to draw these concentric circles of intimacy for ourselves, reflect on where we would place the people currently in our lives and move toward greater awareness about our relationships and greater control of who we wish to keep close.

Go Where You Are Seen

One of the privileges of maturing as women is that we get to a point where we are comfortable with not being close friends with everybody. This can take us years to understand because many of us have been raised to please everyone. However, we need to recognize that when we are not being seen by others as the noble souls we are, it is time to make some adjustments and possibly move on. When we are striving for authentic relationships, we also become more discerning about how we spend our time and who we spend it with. We readily recognize the people who bring out the best in us, and who feels great to be around. We are also aware that some individuals drain our energy or bring out our insecurities. All this is powerful information and would ideally inform our decisions about how and with whom we spend our time. Healer Julie Burns Walker has helped me to understand that if people do not see the nobility in us, then they are not meant to be in our lives in an intimate way. A first step in moving toward greater authenticity in our relationships might therefore be to reflect on the relationships in which we feel seen or valued, and also those in which we do not feel understood. We can then decide to spend our time where we feel seen.

Seek Spiritual Mentors

Our souls have the need to be seen, to love and to be loved, and it is up to us to strive to meet these needs in healthy ways that cultivate the growth of our souls and elevate our nobility. One strategy for doing this is to seek spiritual mentors. We are accustomed to the idea of seeking mentors who are successful in the ways we wish to be successful in our careers or creative endeavors. What we pay less attention to is the fact that we are drawn to people who would serve as mentors not only because of their success, but also because they embody many of the soul attributes we admire. We have an instinctive recognition that by putting ourselves in close proximity with an individual who has shown enough courage or determination to overcome certain obstacles, we might learn to do the same. In seeking mentors we are essentially putting ourselves in a position to learn through their example about the daily lived experience of manifesting creativity, joy, confidence, humility and truthfulness. We are open to learning how our mentors make decisions, what motivates them and what inspires them. We can therefore think of mentors in our professions and entrepreneurship as also being spiritual mentors who consistently manifest attributes of the soul.

The power of example in facilitating change has been noted by author Jonathan Haidt in his book *The Righteous Mind: Why Good People are Divided by Politics and Religion.* Haidt argues that the primary way people change their minds is by interacting with other people. Using the metaphor of an elephant and an elephant rider to explain the relationship between our emotional brains, the elephant, and our logical brains, the rider, Haidt writes, "if there is affection, admiration, or a desire to please the other person, then the elephant leans *toward* that person and the rider tries to find the truth in the other person's arguments. The elephant may not often change its direction in response to objections from its *own* rider, but it is easily steered by the mere presence of friendly elephants . . . or by the good arguments given to it by the riders of those friendly elephants."[4] We have already discussed in Chapter 2 how, as women, we have the gifts of being able to make connections with others and nurture friendships. We can use these gifts, and the principle of the power of example, to facilitate the growth of our souls by seeking mentors whose attributes inspire us, and by becoming more intentional about who we choose to spend our time with.

Let Go of a Scarcity Mindset

Patriarchy, in its devaluation of women, has forced us into a scarcity mindset. Our awareness that women are not valued has meant we feel we have to compete with one another for attention and approval which we perceive are limited resources. We need to recognize that any competition is buying into a myth of scarcity that has us thinking we are not enough, and that we have to engage in the process of acquiring value. The truth is that each of us has a unique expression of the gifts that are needed for society to move forward. We are enough just as we are. If we could move past a scarcity mindset where someone else's success means there is less for us, or that our own success means someone else must be losing out, we would all have a saner and more tranquil existence. Through prayer and meditation we can increase our assurance that the universe will deliver everything meant for us according to its perfect timing.

Beware the Barriers Within

Becoming more authentic also requires us to recognize and evolve any patterns of thought and behavior that prevent us from seeing the nobility of others. There are a number of internal barriers to authentic relationships that are not the unique purview of women but are, nevertheless, ones we must address because they get in the way of engaging authentically with others. These include prejudice, separation, competition and the stories we tell ourselves about who we are. Let us look at how we might address each of these internal barriers to establishing authentic relationships in turn.

Eliminate Prejudice

A key barrier to authentic relationships is prejudice. Prejudice means judging before we have full information. Prejudice is inauthentic because it does not acknowledge the other's nobility and it makes us blind to truth.

When I came to the United States from Kenya, I moved from a society steeped in tribalism to a society steeped in racism, and although both are forms of prejudice they are different. In her *New York Times* bestselling book *So You Want to Talk About Race,* Ijeoma Oluo defines racism as "any prejudice against someone because of their race, when those views are reinforced by systems of power."[5] This definition encompasses the systemic nature of racism in the U.S. and means individuals do not have to be racist to be part of a racist system.

Isabel Wilkerson says that racism in the United States "dates to the start of the transatlantic slave trade and thus to the subsequent caste system that arose from slavery."[6] Describing research on the human genome, Wilkerson goes on to say that there are no biological underpinnings or genetic markers to buttress the concept of race and that race is a social construct. Referencing the work of Professor Ashley Montagu, Wilkerson further states that, "the idea of race was . . . the deliberate creation of an exploiting class seeking to maintain and defend its privileges against what was profitably regarded as an inferior caste."[7]

Racism in the U.S. is sustained by both individual attitudes and the structures of society, and must therefore be addressed at these two levels. Addressing structural racism is beyond the scope of this book, but racism as it is manifested by individuals is the very antithesis of authenticity and must be rooted out if we are to have any chance at authentic relationships with anyone.

When it comes to the individual changes we must all make to address racism, recognizing the ways we are participating in a racist system is key. When we moved back to the U.S. from Abu Dhabi and were deciding where to live, our key focus was to be in a town that had good schools. In doing so, we bought into a history of unequal access to wealth and resources created by racist policies such as redlining, in which banks refused home loans to individuals in some neighborhoods based on race and ethnicity.[8]

I am still learning about what will help us rid ourselves of the scourge of racism as I navigate life in the U.S., and I believe the changes we are hoping for with all our hearts must be about spiritual transformation. My own reckoning with the tribalism I was taught as a child and my willingness to acknowledge and change my behavior was the result of a change of heart. It was a change at the spiritual level about how I viewed myself and others. My tribalism began to crumble when I lifted my loyalty from tribe to human family. I needed to become more committed to the reality that all human souls are part of one human family than to the otherizing I had been taught. Can we shift racism as it manifests at the individual level in a similar way?

Can we begin to address racism by lifting our loyalty to a higher level? Rather than buying into ways of thinking that result in oppression and separation, let us look at the deeper truth of who we are as souls. Can we honor all human beings for what they are: noble and radiant souls, here to grow their attributes and contribute to society through service?

Let us also all do the work we can to create communities and a society in which everyone can achieve their potential. I often think that building inclusive communities must be part of the solution. In the United States our houses are built close to each other, but in some neighborhoods we don't know who lives next door. Let's begin to change that. My heart sinks when my son tells me he is going out for a jog, and I know he would be safer in my town and community if people knew him as a kind and humble young man longing to serve humanity. If, at the neighborhood level, we connect and support one another in raising our families we can begin to build the kinds of societies we hope for.

Expand Our Circles

Being in an authentic relationship with humanity means being willing to take people into our inner circles who are very different from us. This is one way we can move past the prejudices we have been taught or have absorbed from the world around us. Relationships, associations, clubs and meetings that are exclusive are by nature inauthentic. The separation of society in the U.S. is a clear barrier to moving beyond prejudice. Looking at cross-race relationships, the Pew Research Foundation states that, "Among adults who are white with no other race in their background, fully 81 percent say that all or most of their close friends are white. Among single-race blacks, 70 percent say that all or most of their close friends are black. And among single-race Asians, 54 percent say that most of their close friends are Asian."[9]

We can start to move the needle on this separation by asking ourselves who is invited to dinner at our homes. Has a person of another race, religion, culture or ethnicity ever been inside our house? As women in particular, we can do a lot to shape our children's thinking by being inclusive and connecting with people of all backgrounds. Who are our friends? Do our friendships cross racial lines? Our children are watching and learning from us.

In some spheres of American society, there is what I have come to call a "window shopping" relationship with diversity. We like that our towns look diverse when we walk down the street, but that is as far as it goes. We can only truly witness each other's noble souls if we come into contact with one another. We must therefore ask ourselves what the barriers are within us that prevent us from relating to people of all backgrounds. Whatever these are, they also stand in the way of our own complete manifestation as noble souls. In this sphere, I have learned a lot from two close friends of mine who have a special gift for being inclusive. Whenever I attend a party at their homes, I notice there are people from across the globe present and the gatherings feel warm and welcoming. Perhaps we can all strive to open our homes to people of all backgrounds.

Give Up Competition

When I first came across the idea that human beings have intrinsic value—that we have value because *we are* and not because of anything we do—I don't think I fully understood it. In some ways it sounded like a foreign language because I was too caught up in a life of seeking value outside myself by doing well in school and later performing well at work. I was not conscious of any desire to be valued, but I realize with hindsight that as a girl child in a culture that clearly valued males over females, I was set on a path of seeking approval. I thought I needed to earn my value, which led to a pattern of academic competitiveness.

Competitiveness is the bane of modern life, and is a direct result of thinking that our value as human beings is outside ourselves. We falsely believe that we gain value from what we do, how we look, and how much we accomplish. We also believe that when we do any of these things better than others, we have more value. Nothing could be further from the truth.

In *Love, Power and Justice: The Dynamics of Authentic Morality*, Professor Hatcher argues that if our goal is to win any competition, the surest way to ensure this is to sabotage our opponents, and that a more constructive way to foster our own growth is to pursue excellence.[10] This means developing our talents and capacities to their full potential not relative to someone else, but as a manifestation of all we can possibly be. In the pursuit of excellence, we seek not to be better than someone else, but to be better than we were yesterday. Our last performance at anything becomes the reference point, and not what someone else is doing.

A conversation I had with a client will illustrate this. Erica was an aspiring musician and a very talented violinist; she was also seeking treatment for anorexia. After several sessions, Erica's symptoms were significantly reduced, and we were able to address some of the underlying emotional patterns that were driving the eating disorder. In one of her sessions, she disclosed that she was very worried about another girl in the school orchestra Erica believed was better than she was at violin, and how the tryouts for a select string quartet "are stressing me out, because she can do amazing things with the violin."

"Well, you know the one thing that will guarantee things go your way for the tryouts is to find a way to meddle with her violin, so it doesn't work," I offered, drawing directly from the work of Professor Hatcher.

Erica looked shocked, "What?"

"If your goal is to be better than her, the surest way to win is to sabotage her in some way."

Erica drew her eyes together in a questioning frown, and waited for me to continue.

"Well, let's think about this. Is your goal to be better than Janet or is your goal to be the best violinist you can be?"

With no hesitation, Erica replied, "To be the best violinist I can be."

"So then let's say, for example, you have the talent to be playing at Carnegie Hall someday. Because your focus is just beating Janet, once you do that you may stop striving for excellence and never discover how good you can get."

"Oh—I get it!" Erica started laughing.

"However, let's say both you and Janet were aiming to be the best violinists you could be, then the world would be richer and better for it."

"Yes, and you know what? String quartets have two violins anyway," Erica smiled.

Many of the women who find their way to my office are successful career women, high-achieving students and talented athletes and musicians. They hold themselves to high standards, which in itself is not a problem. However, they continue to feel empty regardless of their accomplishments because they are in competition for value with others. Let us replace competing against each other with the pursuit of excellence, and become the noble souls we were intended to be.

Challenge Your Story

Among the internal barriers to authenticity are the false beliefs we hold and untrue stories we tell ourselves. Often we harbor ideas and ways of thinking that we have been taught and accept them without questioning. We also place limitations on ourselves that may have come from others. Allowing ourselves to examine our beliefs with honesty and compassion helps us to dismantle false ideas. We can let go of beliefs that prevent us from manifesting our full potential. A simple, "Now where did I learn that?" or "Who taught me that?" will start us off on a process of thinking through which beliefs about ourselves are based in reality.

I have noticed a tendency among my clients who have had negative childhood experiences to see the past as all bad. As we take stock of our stories and find areas we need to adapt and change, we also need to be aware that there are many positive aspects of our experiences we must keep and strengthen. In the midst of chaos and suffering, there was a friend, a parent, a grandmother, an aunt or a teacher who saw us as individuals with great potential and reflected this to us enough that we made it through to today. Being able to see both the positive and the negative influences in our past supports us in our pursuit of authenticity.

At their core, authentic relationships are those in which we recognize the noble qualities in others and treat them in ways that are consistent with their nobility and our own. As Nobuko's treatment progressed, she reported she felt less competitive with her peers and less fixated on her body weight. She was moving toward greater authenticity with herself and with others. In the next chapter we will discuss the role of challenges and difficulties in our spiritual growth.

TO GO DEEPER

Building Capacity for Authentic Relationships

Having defined authenticity and authentic relationships, and explored the internal barriers that contribute to inauthenticity, you may want to explore ways to become more authentic and cultivate authentic relationships. Here are a few pointers for your journey.

1. NOTICE THE POSITIVE ATTRIBUTES OF EVERYONE AROUND YOU

Practice seeing the attributes in others and acknowledge them for it. Start with simple statements such as, "That was very courageous" or, "Thank you for your generosity." Recognizing and calling another soul to their attributes is the essence of authenticity.

2. CONFRONT INTERNALIZED PREJUDICE AND RACISM

What have you been taught that might have led to conscious or even subconscious prejudice? How do people you know talk about people who are different, about gender, race, ethnicity, or class? Challenge yourself to see things without the veil of prejudice. A good place to start might be to increase your awareness by writing down ways you are participating in a racist system. What things can you do easily that might not be available to people of other races? You might also note down if you are not comfortable meeting with people from certain groups or inviting them into your home. With this awareness, you can begin to make changes.

3. CELEBRATE OTHERS' VICTORIES

Move away from a culture of competition by celebrating the successes and victories of others. Do you acknowledge people for their success? Give someone encouraging feedback about their achievements. For example, you can celebrate a friend who got the promotion she was seeking, or send an encouraging note to a friend whose business is going well.

4. DROP THE VICTIM STORY

Is there a story you are telling yourself about your life that keeps you in victim mode? Do you give others power to determine your circumstances and your happiness? Be honest about where you are and take charge of the journey toward fulfilling your potential. A first step might be to write down ways you make excuses for yourself, or ways you blame others for your predicament. You can then review what you have written and come up with alternatives that give you the power to make changes. For example, "I am miserable because my mother loved my sister more" can become "I can be kind to myself and cultivate loving relationships."

Recollections:
The Grief of the World

The phone rings at 12:40 a.m. on August 17, 2020 and I know it is sad news. My sister just passed away in a hospital in Nairobi. Both my parents are deceased, so my uncles, aunts and cousins mobilize themselves to do all that is necessary for the funeral. I cannot travel because of the Covid-19 pandemic, so I join the daily family meetings to organize the funeral program by phone. There are some heart-wrenching decisions to make, including holding the funeral without all family members present because of quarantine requirements. I become a night owl so I can attend the meetings by phone from the U.S. I am grateful for the strength of our extended family and all my relatives' support and commitment to giving my sister a beautiful send-off. I watch the funeral with my husband via livestream. My heart is full of the deepest gratitude for my cousins, uncles and aunts.

A cousin sends me a text message commending me for the way I handled issues and remained calm during the lead-up to my sister's funeral. I am moved by the message; it feels good to be acknowledged for the gifts I bring. I also notice that my relationship with this acknowledgement is very different from the desperate desire for approval that plagued my childhood, youth and young adulthood. I am more independent, and I enjoy the compliment while knowing it does not make me any more worthy than I am already. I also see that my cousin's acknowledgement says more about his nobility than it does about mine, and I am grateful to be related to such a kind soul. It has been a long, long journey to this point.

Months have passed since my sister's death, but my grief feels overwhelming and exhausting. It is much deeper and heavier than I was expecting. One night I have a dream in which I see a woman sitting on a tree stump in the distance, and I walk to her through what seems like a cool, white morning mist hovering over the earth. When I reach her, I see her gray hair is covered with a blue headscarf that also drapes over her shoulders. She smiles at me and tells me not to have a heavy heart. She also tells me I am not just grieving my sister, but I am also grieving for all women. Somehow I am not surprised she knows about my sister. She says I am wondering what women need to do to be seen and acknowledged for what they bring to the world. She tells me it will take time to heal and I should be gentle with myself. I wake up and feel like it was an important dream. The woman's words make sense because what I am holding feels very heavy. I resolve to take some time to rest, and I feel grateful for the guidance I received in the dream.

My intention is to write this book, but getting into the chair to do the work seems impossible. I feel like I am trying to walk through molasses and I just cannot make myself write. I clean the house, reorganize the basement, clean the deck—anything to delay the writing. It seems I am a master procrastinator, but I also know that there is more to this difficulty with writing

*than that. I pray about it and an image drops into my con-
sciousness. I am surprised at its clarity because I have never
experienced anything like this before. It is the image of a sick
woman lying on a mat. She has a red-and-green cloth wrapped
around her body, her hair is short like mine and her arms are
very weak. It comes to me that she has been left to die because
she speaks her mind. She is one of my ancestors, and she has
been trying to protect me from the consequences of telling my
story because the repercussions of having a voice and speaking
up have been dire for the women who have gone before me. I
feel a deep sadness for this woman and I pray for her healing.
While I pray, I feel the support of my female ancestors and I
am both happy and humbled by this experience of connection
with them. It becomes easier to write.*

CHAPTER 7

Lean into Hardship

M y heart skipped a beat when I saw the pale-blue air-mail envelope lying on the top of my in-tray, and I put down my briefcase before picking it up. The handwriting on the envelope was familiar and even as I opened it I knew that one of my dearest friends from college was telling me she was getting married. I was happy for her as I read the letter, but I also felt a flood of sadness rising in me. I needed to go to the ladies' room before the glass partitioning to my office revealed a weeping mess. The path was clear, and in the privacy of a toilet cubicle I allowed tears to flow as I felt the heartbreak of my most recent romantic disappointment. I wondered if I would ever meet my person. Knowing a brave face was needed to get on with the work day, I composed myself by drawing on my faith and reminding myself not to lose my trust in the bounties of God. I took some deep breaths, washed my hands, wiped away some running mascara and walked back into the office. There was nothing remarkable about the rest of that work day. I do not recall any of the meetings, phone calls or any of the projects I worked on, but I do remember that at about 4:00 p.m., a friend of mine called to invite me to an impromptu gathering at her house. I was grateful to have a distraction for the evening and gladly accepted. While I was at her home, a young man I had not met before arrived.

Our eyes met and I could tell we were both intrigued with one another. I did not know it at the time, but that was the evening I met my husband. That man was and is my person, and we married seven months after meeting. I am still in awe of the fact that my husband showed up in my life on the same day I had consciously reminded myself to trust in the bounties of God.

I remember exactly what I was wearing that day because of the personal work I was doing to figure out life and heal from a messy relationship. I had listened to a tape on intimate relationships in which the speaker asked the listeners to make a list of all the characteristics of their ideal partners, and then dropped a bomb that still makes me laugh by asking if your ideal partner would date you.[1] I had fully embraced the recommendation that my focus needed to be on becoming the person my ideal partner would be drawn to. For me, that looked like a confident woman with a refined presence and elegant clothes. On the evening I met my husband, I was not the weepy mess I had been earlier in the day. Instead I was standing in power and feeling on point in a long brown dress with a beautiful drape, bronze pumps and freshly styled hair.

More than twenty years later, I can look back at the disappointments I experienced in the relationships I had before I met my husband with some objectivity. It now seems to me that growth from hardships might happen in two ways: we get some hints of light as we are actually going through the struggle, and we develop a fuller understanding after the fact. When I was going through heartbreak my mind was in such turmoil. Why wasn't I good enough? What could I have done better or differently to make things work? Will I ever meet someone special? I pushed through days at work and in the evenings I would see friends who would try to cheer me up and give me hope. I would cry at night, and then wake up in the morning to force myself through another day. I would pray and feel fleeting moments of comfort, but the days felt long and the months to come loomed over me like dark, gray clouds. Now, many years later, I can look back and think to myself that things worked out for the best, and I can see that my disappointments deepened my faith and trust in the Creator. I may have felt less despair if I had trusted in the moment that the pain I was experiencing would lead to my growth. The perfectionist tendencies of my ego sometimes tempt me to think that if I was able to appreciate that the tears, confusion and crises of confidence would lead me to where I am today, perhaps at the time I might have seen those difficult emotions and the heartbreak of failed relationships as the gifts they actually were. However, I see now that the path of spiritual growth is one filled with tribulation, that sometimes we get to hold onto hope with a very thin thread, and this can be all our souls need to move forward.

A Missing Narrative

In my line of work, I see clients because some aspect of their lives is challenging or distressing. Many of them have underlying assumptions about how life is supposed to unfold. These assumptions often contribute to their distress. Somehow, we have bought into the illusion that life is supposed to be easy. This notion is the source of much of the anguish we experience when we face difficulties. If we are not living out our imagined ideal lives, we conclude that there is something wrong with us, that we haven't found the right life strategy or that we are not living to purpose.

That life is supposed to be easy is a false narrative. To replace it with a more accurate and more helpful one, we need to revisit our understanding of who we are and why we are here. In Chapter 3 we discussed our true identities as noble souls, and in Chapter 4 we looked at how each human being has a physical and a spiritual nature. We also considered how the primary purpose of the physical nature is to serve the development of our souls. We live on Earth for a period of growth and at the moment of death, we pass into the next existence with the spiritual capacities and attributes our souls have developed.

The purpose of our time here then is to develop our attributes: the love, courage, patience and determination that are the beautiful facets of each of our souls. So how do these attributes grow and develop in the course of our lives? Just as our muscles grow in strength as we use them, we become more loving by showing love and become more aware of when it is required of us. Our attributes also grow through adversity. We do not, for example, become more patient in a vacuum. Our patience needs to be challenged if we are to develop our capacity for it. Our patience grows when we take deep breaths and avoid swearing or angrily honking the horn when someone cuts in front of us in traffic. Author Luvvie Ajayi Jones reminds us in her book *Professional Troublemaker: The Fear-Fighter Manual* that we often manifest courage when we are faced with fear.[2] Our spiritual growth lies in the space between the challenges we face and our capacity to overcome them. Our true growth, the growth of the attributes of our souls, happens as a result of hardship, difficulty and challenge. These hardships are like the air we breathe. They are an integral and necessary part of our existence. The missing narrative in modern Western culture is that life is *supposed* to be challenging.

Problematic Narratives

Not only have we been navigating life with a missing narrative, we have also been taught narratives that actually put us at a disadvantage when it comes to dealing with hardship.

In his book *Life Changing Conversations,* Dr. Jon Connelly attributes our lack of preparation for dealing with adversity in Western culture to the fact we grow up with the myth that if we are good, good things will happen or "things are good if you are good."[3] This perspective is taught early in many stories we read to our children, the films they watch, and also through rituals around gifts and monetary rewards for good behavior. In Connelly's training sessions he illustrates the problematic nature of this view using the example of children being encouraged to behave because Santa sees them and will bring them toys on Christmas Eve as a reward for their good behavior. The idea that good actions beget good things does not prepare anyone for the loss of a home in a natural disaster, or the loss of a parent in a car accident.

A corollary of the narrative that good behavior leads to reward is that unfortunate or tragic circumstances are caused by bad behavior. This leads to further distress when faced with difficulties, and it can also make us judgmental about other people's predicaments. If we have been trained at the subconscious level to think that good things happen to good people, we automatically think that people in difficult circumstances must deserve their hardship because they have not been good enough to merit rewards or a good life. The mind that has accepted inaccurate narratives about the causes of difficulties does not have the tools or perspectives needed to navigate life well.

Reframing Our Relationship with Difficulties

Our spiritual traditions teach us that suffering and distress can lead to spiritual growth and positive change. Psychology also recognizes posttraumatic growth as a phenomenon in which difficulty and distress lead to higher levels of functioning than were experienced prior to the hardship. Following tragic events, individuals who experience post-traumatic growth demonstrate positive changes in personality including greater optimism, positive affect or emotion and greater satisfaction with social supports.[4]

We also know an individual's emotional response to a traumatic event determines the long-term impact of trauma. It seems obvious, therefore, that the perspective we have about the role of challenges and difficulties in our lives would affect our response to traumatic events and therefore our mental health. We might find life much easier if we acknowledge that our challenges strengthen us even while we are experiencing them. We need to understand that in this existence we are supposed to be tested. Reframing our understanding regarding difficulties will change our relationship with challenges, transform the ways we tackle difficulties and impact our mental health in positive ways. Rather than resisting challenges, we can seek to understand the wisdom of the challenges we are facing. We can lean into hardship even as it is happening. Perhaps we might even welcome difficulty, knowing that while it is a storm in our lives it also offers growth, drawing us closer to our Source and leaving us with greater wisdom and stronger character. We can consider this world as the workshop within which we undergo all the transformation and refinement we need to develop our spiritual attributes.

And for the Brave but Wise . . .

The process of producing a gleaming, multifaceted diamond provides a helpful analogy for understanding how our character's refinement requires testing. In the raw, a diamond looks like a rock. To the expert eye though, there is potential beauty in the rock. Producing a finished gem from its raw state is not a gentle process. Cutting, grinding and polishing are all rough actions that bring out the gleaming facets of a precious stone. Similarly, the beautiful facets of our souls—our attributes—need the hardships and difficulties of our lives to truly shine. The greater our commitment to spiritual growth, the more open we become to the burdens that bring out our inner beauty.

If we understand the purpose of our lives is to grow spiritually and difficulties are the cause of growth, we might actually wish for more hardship in our lives. I am very content dealing with the tests that come my way and cannot imagine wishing for more, but I wanted to mention this option so I do not transfer my limitations to you. If you are so enamored by your spiritual growth and your connection with your Source that you feel inclined to wish for difficulties, please feel free to do so!

That said, it is a good idea to avoid self-inflicted tests. The universe has no trouble coming up with the tests we need for our growth, and does not need any help from us. There is a difference between the tests that are brought to us to facilitate our growth and the difficulties that we create for ourselves by not living according to our high station as noble souls.

Finding Meaning in the Struggle

Accompanying clients to heal and recover from eating disorders has taught me much about the resilience of women. One aspect of treatment is recognizing the social forces that contribute to the development of disease, as illustrated in this conversation with my client Zainab, a wonderful woman in her early forties seeking treatment for bulimia.

"When I got injured and could not go to the gym, I felt I lost control of everything. That's when the vomiting started."

"And at the time you were thinking . . . " I invited her to continue.

"I was thinking that if I got rid of the food, I would not gain weight."

"Gaining weight was not something you wanted because . . . "

"How I feel about myself has a lot to do with my body."

"Where did you learn that?"

"Oh, just everywhere. There's so much about how we should look as women, I guess."

Zainab and I continued to discuss the social messages that pervade our society including advertising which focuses on making women appear as perfect as possible. We talked about how seeing through these pressures and making independent decisions about our true identity is the beginning of freedom. We also discussed how developing an eating disorder affords us the opportunity to critically examine societal messages and increase our autonomy as women. We explored how eating disorders can open women's eyes to the pressures society places on us and the impact of these pressures on our lives. Zainab became more open to considering new truths about who she is and rejecting the standards society imposes on women.

No Matter the Struggle

The challenges we face vary significantly, but we are all tested. For some of us, the difficulties in life will be of a physical nature, for example meeting our daily needs for shelter and food. When I work with clients for whom housing support and finding jobs are the key challenges, overcoming those tests and finding the support and resources available in the community is the focus. For others, the tests are different. Perhaps they involve the anguish and shame of being bullied or abused, or the low self-esteem that results from demeaning messages. Many face tests and difficulties like physical illness and disease. Whatever the nature of the tests we encounter in life, we can be confident that their ultimate outcome is the development of our spiritual capacities and attributes. We can trust that everything we face is needed to help us advance to the next stage of our development.

Regardless of the difficulties we encounter, having the mindset that tests are for our development gives meaning to our lives. Asking ourselves what attributes we need to exhibit even as things are falling apart around us allows us to consciously grow our qualities. Instead of being swept up in the chaos of whatever the challenge is, we remain grounded in knowing our purpose is to grow as spiritual beings. If we are here to grow, and we know we grow most when we are facing challenges, we would expect life would, by design, put all the challenges we need before us. Contrary to popular belief, we are not here to be happy or comfortable; rather, we are here to grow, and that is not an easy journey. However, the difficulties we encounter in life lead to our spiritual growth and ultimately to a true happiness that is independent of our circumstances in life.

And When You Notice You Are on Repeat . . .

It is not uncommon to find ourselves navigating the same difficulty over and over. We might also notice the themes of seemingly different situations are strikingly similar. For example, we continue to have friends who seek us out when they need something, but are not there for us; we sabotage our efforts toward our goals or our relationships just when they seem to be going well; or we relate to everyone as if they are the source of our trauma. In *The Wisdom of No Escape,* Pema Chödrön writes, "You can leave your marriage, you can quit your job, you can only go where people are going to praise you, you can manipulate your world until you're blue in the face to try to make it always smooth, but the same old demons will always come up until finally you have learned your lesson, the lesson they came to teach you. Then those same demons will appear as friendly, warmhearted companions on the path."[5]

When we approach difficulties with the knowledge that a key purpose of our lives is to grow spiritually, we will reduce our need for multiple life experiences to teach us the same thing. If we lean into hardship by looking for the wisdom and lessons from the beginning, we become more efficient at learning from each experience. One of the dynamics of our spiritual development is that the same tests come to us, sometimes becoming more intense until we have learned our lesson. For example, our growth may require us to relinquish a victimhood story we have long held dear, and we continue to be tested until we can let it go.

In *The Power of Now*, Eckhart Tolle warns us of relating to life through the pain body or the places where we are hurt or injured, and reminds us that our growth happens as we relinquish our preciously guarded pain bodies.[6] When one particular place of vulnerability is transformed into a place of strength, we will pass that area of testing and graduate to a new kind of test. Tests continue as long as we are on this earth.

Much of what we know of the role of difficulties in our lives has come to us in the sacred writings of the world's spiritual traditions. Poets and authors have also contributed to our understanding and invited us to see that our pain and joy are related. In his book *The Prophet,* Kahlil Gibran reminds us that, "The selfsame well from which your laughter rises was oftentimes filled with your tears."[7] In the poem "Childhood Friends," Rumi tells us, "Don't turn your head. Keep looking at the bandaged place. This is where the light enters you."[8] Let us stay committed to knowing that no matter how much we are struggling, the light will follow.

Living with the understanding that life is meant to be challenging and that these challenges are there to foster our growth is a mindset that can reduce suffering. As Glennon Doyle, activist and author of *Untamed*, writes, "I am a human being, meant to be in perpetual becoming. If I am living bravely, my entire life will become a million deaths and rebirths. My goal is not to remain the same but to live in such a way that each day, year, moment, relationship, conversation, and crisis is the material I use to become a truer, more beautiful version of myself."[9]

I notice that I have gradually emerged as a truer version of myself as I have shed the many false messages I internalized as result of being born and raised in a society that considered me less than because I came to Earth to experience life as female. With hindsight I also see that the disappointments I faced in relationships before I met my husband have taught me lessons that have made me stronger and that I can share with others when needed. While I sometimes remind myself to seek the wisdom and find the lessons while I am facing challenges or difficulties, I don't always get there, and I accept my humanity.

So far in our journey together we have looked at the attributes of our souls, the duality of human nature and our purpose. We have also considered the key principles of authentic relationships and reframed our understanding of tests and difficulties. In the next chapter we will explore what we can do on a daily basis to foster our spiritual growth and the development of our noble souls.

TO GO DEEPER

Learning What Hardship Has to Teach Us

We have reflected on how hardships and difficulties contribute to our growth. Here are some questions for reflection to facilitate your awareness on growing through hardship.

1. KNOW THAT YOU ARE HERE TO BE TESTED

What attitudes do you currently hold about hardship and difficulties? What have you noticed about how those attitudes influence how you navigate your tests? Would you be willing to reconsider the purpose of difficulties in your life? As a first step, you might wish to write down one or two of the most recent challenges you have faced, and also make some notes on how you handled them. Now write down how you would have approached the same challenges if you knew that you are on Earth to be tested and to grow.

2. TAKE STOCK OF YOUR GROWTH THROUGH TRIALS

If we take a moment to consider some of the challenges we have experienced, we might notice they caused us to take a different direction or meet someone or do something that put us on an entirely different course. Write down two of the most significant challenges or difficulties you have faced in your life. As you look back at each of these challenges, list the ways in which facing these challenges caused you to grow. Think about and list the attributes you needed to draw on to navigate the hardship or difficulty.

3. HAVE THE DESIRED OUTCOME IN MIND AT THE BEGINNING

Think back to the last major challenge you faced. Note down any of the thoughts you remember having as you were going through it. Next, list ways in which you grew from experiencing this difficulty. Now reflect on how you might have approached the challenge if you knew you would grow from the experience.

Recollections:
Learning the Power of Prayer

It is a hot Ohio morning and I am pushing my son in a blue stroller around the apartment complex where we live. He is a happy baby and brings me much joy. My son falls asleep and I return to our apartment. I leave him in the stroller just inside our front door. I make tea and sit for a few minutes. My life is filled with sweet moments taking care of my little one, but it is also isolating. Ohio is so different from Nairobi and I feel disconnected and uncertain about everything. With no one to turn to and a long day ahead before my husband comes home, prayer is all I have. I pick up a prayer book. I beseech God to send me a friend, "You know I don't need many friends, just one will do."

A few weeks later, I am sitting on the floor of the playroom at my newly found friend's home. She has two daughters and her youngest is a little older than my son. We talk about our lives as mothers, and she tells me about attachment parenting and homeschooling. I am intrigued. I buy one of the books she recommends and find in it an approach to parenting that feels so much better than what our pediatrician recommended. We add a single bed to the queen-sized one already in our bedroom. We now have a wall-to-wall bed, and the whole family gets a little more sleep each night.

My new friend introduces me to one of her friends and soon I am part of a circle of supportive women who see me through a miscarriage and deliver soup when I am too busy caring for a toddler to notice my deteriorating health. They also gently tell me that the bleeding I am experiencing is not normal and urge me to see a doctor.

Looking back to those days in Ohio, I thank God for really delivering on my prayer for a friend.

It is April 2020, and the number of Covid-19 cases at the hospital where my husband works is rising each day. My daughter and son are both home from college and it is sweet to be together. We have conversations about the possibility of their dad getting sick and us not being able to see him. It is hard to keep my mind from going to all kinds of what-ifs. What if he gets the virus? What if he brings it home and our children get sick? What if my husband and I both die and our children are left without parents? I recognize my mind is not in a good place, and I do the one thing I know will help. I pray. My prayers for protection for my husband, friends and all others on the frontline are urgent. Some moments after I stop praying, a quiet knowing settles gently in my being, almost like a rose petal floating through the air to land softly on the grass. It comes to me that all the learning and training my husband has been through was to make him ready for moments like this. Helping the sick is his calling and he is now doing what he was created to do. My fear and anxiety are replaced with gratitude for what my husband and everyone on the frontline are doing.

After eight weeks navigating a bizarre allergic reaction in the summer of 2021, I still do not know what caused it. To sustain my health I have eliminated most of the foods I rely on. The rash that covers many parts of my body has me worried about sun exposure, so I am no longer taking my regular walks, and restless nights have me waking up later than usual in the mornings. I feel disoriented, and wonder how to get back on track. It occurs to me to start with the basics. I wake up and make a point of praying and meditating. The day goes better. I do the same the next day, and the day after that. I start to feel like myself again. I am grateful that when I lose my way, I can start again. I see spiritual practice is exactly that—practice. I can restart at any time because the journey of spiritual growth is always beginning.

CHAPTER 8

Develop a Spiritual Practice

" Don't you love that wherever we start with a client, at some point their journey becomes about spirit?" This was the reflection of one of my colleagues in the healing arts, and I have heard many clients express some form of, "Now that I am stronger in recovery, what should I do with my life?" or "My trauma is cleared, now what?" These kinds of questions point us in the direction of opening the door to our spiritual growth. Magic happens when we start to entertain questions about what it means to be a human and we consciously engage on a journey of spiritual growth and the development of our souls. This was the case with Elizabeth, a young woman in her mid-twenties seeking relief from emotional pain. Her life had been eventful: she was bullied in elementary school; her high school boyfriend physically abused her; her father had physically abused both Elizabeth and her mother; and she had used opiates to cope with her pain. As Elizabeth's trauma cleared in the course of her treatment, she mentioned she was feeling better than she had in years. Soon after this, in what I anticipated would be her last session, Elizabeth reviewed the progress she had made in therapy. Toward the end of the session, she said, "I feel I am on a spiritual journey. Can you guide me?"

We spent the remainder of that session reviewing what Elizabeth was already doing to nurture her soul, and what she felt was missing. Elizabeth stated she felt she was spiritual, but she did not know how to "move forward with this." She also said she was looking for a community of people who thought like her and that she had started going to a local church. I applauded Elizabeth for taking this step, and encouraged her to keep going and to trust herself as she continued to seek what she needed.

In this chapter we will consider the practical steps we can take to embark on or deepen our journey of spiritual growth and ensure we manifest as the noble souls we are intended to be. We have, of course, considered some of these steps toward spiritual growth in the earlier parts of the book. Here, we will be putting them together as elements of a practice through which we proactively foster our spiritual growth in our daily lives. We will discuss the importance of finding a spiritual path, daily habits for nurturing our souls, taking a dynamic view of our spiritual growth and living in the spiritual dimension. We will consider each of these key elements of spiritual growth separately for clarity's sake, while acknowledging that all of these elements are interconnected and that any effort we make in one area will reinforce the others.

Find a Spiritual Path

Given what we know about the benefits of spirituality to our well-being and mental health, finding a spiritual path that resonates with us would not only help us grow spiritually, but would also enhance our well-being and mental health. Fortunately, we have options. A number of paths have been available to humanity over time through the traditions of native peoples, and through the revelations that have come through Moses, Abraham, Krishna, Zoroaster, Buddha, Jesus Christ, Muhammad and Baháʼuʼlláh. Following any one of these spiritual paths would support us in developing our souls. Those of us already on a path we are happy with can continue to follow it and deepen our understanding and connection to it. If we are not on a spiritual path we are happy with, we would benefit from investigating others to find one that offers a meaningful approach toward spiritual growth.

Ironically, many of us have lost our way trying to find a spiritual path. Historically, we tended to have our spiritual paths defined for us by our parents, and their paths were defined by their parents. What I have observed in my office is that this system of inheriting a spiritual path from our parents has, for the most part, broken down. When I ask clients at their first appointment if they have any spiritual beliefs, I hear answers like, "I was raised X, but I don't really believe it" or "I used to be X, but I was disappointed with it." Some of us have been eager to distance ourselves from the mess that human beings have made of religion, and in the process we have lost out on the benefits of having a spiritual path. It is true that in the name of religion, humanity has fought wars, oppressed and persecuted entire populations and abused individuals. We cannot, however, confuse the pure intention of the original teachings of these faiths with the tragedies that have been wrought to maintain power or personal gain in their name. Even when we reject the path our parents are on for good reason, we do ourselves a disservice if we do not attempt to find our own. We must acknowledge there is still value in the belief that there is an intangible part of who we are that seeks connection with its Source.

The guidance I offered Elizabeth was to continue her exploration of the church she had started attending, and to engage with its community. If we decide to join any faith community in our search for a spiritual path—as we study holy texts or scripture, meet with members of the community, participate in community life and engage in the daily acts of spiritual discipline prescribed to its followers—we will gain useful information to guide us. It is important we do not engage or suspend engagement with a spiritual path based on someone else's experience. Trusting ourselves as we seek to independently engage with a spiritual path will lead us to the right one.

We grow the most when we are fully engaged with our spiritual path. When we find ourselves on a path that does not ring true to us, we have the option of investigating another until we find our spiritual home. The cost of not engaging is high, and the act of engaging with an open mind and heart will lead us where we want and need to be.

Some of us are comfortable calling ourselves spiritual, but follow no particular path. This option leaves us needing to define a path for ourselves, borrowing what suits us as individuals from different places. We choose soul-nurturing practices we are comfortable with, and we reject anything that challenges us in any way. We need to understand that a valid spiritual path sometimes requires us to be uncomfortable, and we cannot grow spiritually without moving into some areas of discomfort.

Embracing a path and its spiritual practices like prayer, fasting, giving to those in need and reading holy scriptures enables us to develop a discipline that allows inner or spiritual faculties to grow. Adopting spirituality, but not participating in the framework provided by a spiritual path, is like knowing you want to get strong, buying a gym membership and then driving by the gym without going in. Just as our physical muscles will not strengthen without walking in and lifting weights, so too our spiritual faculties do not grow without the disciplined actions recommended by the faith system we choose.

Build Daily Spiritual Habits

Our spiritual growth requires daily attending. The daily habits which support us in fostering the development of our souls include prayer, meditation, reading spiritual guidance, fasting and reflecting on our progress. Prayer and meditation are fundamental habits of a spiritual life, and studies have shown they improve our mood and well-being.

Developments in science have also allowed us to investigate the impact of these spiritual constructs. For example, MRI studies have shown that when prayers and intentions are sent by healers to distant individuals, their effects are positive.[1] Research is also mounting on the impact of mindfulness meditation on mental health. One study showed, "a short program in mindfulness meditation produces demonstrable effects on brain and immune function."[2] A study of Mindfulness-Based Stress Reduction (MBSR), a widely used mindfulness training program, found that "participation in MBSR is associated with changes in gray matter concentration in brain regions involved in learning and memory processes, emotion regulation, self-referential processing, and perspective taking."[3] Another study of the impact of MBSR in adults diagnosed with Generalized Anxiety Disorder revealed that MBSR reduces stress markers, and may enhance resilience to stress.[4]

We understand the value of providing our physical body with nutritious food for it to function well. Similarly, our souls require spiritual nourishment. A helpful way to think about the role of prayer in our lives is to consider it as nourishment for our souls. We also recognize it would be absurd to suggest that we nourish our physical bodies by eating once or twice a week, and yet we ignore the daily nourishing of our souls with prayer.

When we pray, our souls transcend our daily concerns and move us closer to our Source. In this closeness, we feel more ourselves—more of who and what we are at our core. As a soul makes an effort to reach out to a Source or universe that is all-loving and all-generous, it arrives at a closer understanding of its purpose and true nature.

While praying, we are engaging in a conversation. We share the desires of our hearts, our cares, our concerns, our gratitude through spoken word, song or quiet thought. We express the contents of our hearts, and we need to listen for the answers that come. How many times have we engaged in prayer, asked for what we needed and poured out our hearts to our Creator, to then quickly get up and get on with our day without taking the time to listen to the answers? Thinking about meditation as an opportunity to receive answers and guidance puts us in an open frame of mind to receive what there is for us to know. We can also think of meditation as using our soul like a lens that captures the power of the sun and focuses its light on one point. Meditation comes in many forms, and we can choose whatever feels comfortable to us. Some people find it helpful to use inspiring words or passages from scripture to focus their mind's intention. As women, the habit of meditation also gives us an opportunity to check in with ourselves and to tap into what is true for us. This is a foundational piece in awakening to the feminine powers in each of us.

As a complement to prayer and meditation which encapsulate the two-way conversation that we strive to have daily with our Source, we can also expand our understanding of who we are and what is intended for us with the study of holy texts and their guidance. Reading these inspiring passages provides us with guidance on how to live our lives and, if done in the morning, sets the tone for the day as well as lifting our consciousness to a higher level. When we read inspiring passages at the end of our day, the spiritual guidance informs our dreams.

Another important daily habit that fosters spiritual growth is consciously evaluating how we are doing each day. In Chapter 3 we spoke of the importance of evaluating how we are manifesting the attributes each day. Reviewing this and considering how we would like to do better the following day helps us to become intentional about our spiritual growth and makes us conscious of which attributes we want to develop. If prayer and meditation are completely new to us, our daily practice could be as simple as taking a few minutes at the beginning or the end of the day to think about what we are grateful for. We could also take a walk and appreciate the natural beauty around us.

Take a Dynamic View of Spiritual Development

In a world where we are accustomed to instant results, it is easy to fall into the trap of thinking that our spiritual growth should also happen quickly. However, the development of our souls is a dynamic and incremental process in which our victories build on each other. Instead of thinking about ourselves and our inner state as either good or bad, it helps to think that we are works in progress and in a constant state of change and growth.

When we start to look inside ourselves and acknowledge both our strengths and areas for growth, it is imperative that we take a compassionate view. Any self-critical patterns of thought take us quickly to the dark place of judgment. A useful way to approach consciously evaluating our spiritual development is to think about where we are with gentle understanding, and then love ourselves into the next step of growth. A first step might be to write down ways you think you have changed for the better in the last three months, and also ways you would like to grow in the following three months.

Live in the Right Dimension

Thinkers and writers about the human condition point us to a dimension of life we need to access regularly if we are to find inner peace. Dr. Eben Alexander, neurosurgeon and author of *Proof of Heaven*, speaks of the need to access this spiritual dimension which he says is "a universe characterized above all by love."[5] In *The Gifts of Imperfection*, Brené Brown recommends that we dig deep for wholehearted living and states that this practice involves prayer and meditation,[6] thus inviting us to access a different realm to support ourselves.

The idea of living in the spiritual dimension has the potential to change our lives profoundly. When we consider ourselves spiritual beings living in a material existence, we view the purpose of life in a completely different way. We see that the material aspects of life are to serve the spiritual facets of our lives, and our relationship with what we have, how we spend our time and what we contribute to the world changes.

How do we live with a full awareness of the spiritual dimension of life? We need to recognize we are spiritual beings having a material experience so our souls can grow. This world is our souls' classroom and workshop.

To stay connected to the spiritual dimension as we go about our daily lives, we need to remind ourselves to navigate life with an awareness of our souls and attributes. We must use our sense of inner joy as a confirmation that we are on the right track, and we need to face tests and difficulties as lessons.

Being spiritual does not mean we do not enjoy our lives, nor does it mean we give up pleasures and practice asceticism. It does, however, mean we reframe our relationship to material existence, and we do not let ourselves be defined by material standards.

Spiritual journeys begin by acknowledging the existence of the intangible aspects of reality and the nobility of our souls. We must live in ways that are consistent with our chosen spiritual path. Whether, like my client Elizabeth, you are seeking guidance on how to begin a spiritual journey or are hoping to engage more fully with the path you are already on, the perspectives and daily habits we have discussed will strengthen the awareness of your noble soul and support your spiritual growth.

Opportunity Lies in Each Moment

In this book we have discussed the relationship between spirituality and mental health. We then embarked on learning about our reality as spiritual beings and how to foster our spiritual growth. We explored the attributes of our souls, the duality of human nature, our purpose in life, authenticity in relationships and the meaning of hardship. As we grow spiritually and nurture our souls, let us remember to stand strong in our reality as powerful spiritual beings experiencing life on Earth as women. Each one of us has unique gifts to contribute, which are needed if our civilization is to move forward.

Spiritual growth takes effort, but the fruits of this effort are beautiful and far-reaching. When we recognize ourselves as the noble souls we already are, we will be powerful as women.

As long as we are breathing, we have the capacity to grow spiritually. At whatever stage we find ourselves, and at any given point in our lives, we can make choices that are consistent with our soul's development. We can choose to manifest our attributes and nurture our higher selves, and we can strive to serve others and relate to everyone as the noble being they are. As we navigate the journey of life, there are many opportunities and choices that facilitate the growth of our souls. We need to recognize and take advantage of these opportunities in each day and each moment. Travel well, noble soul!

TO GO DEEPER

Fostering Your Spiritual Growth

In becoming proactive participants in our own journeys of spiritual growth, we take charge of our development and our sense of well-being. Here are two important steps to facilitate this journey.

1. FIND A SPIRITUAL PATH

Find the spiritual path you are willing to engage with. You might read books about different religions and visit nearby spiritual communities or houses of worship. If you are already on a path, consider engaging with it more deeply. Perhaps you can deepen your connection to your path by studying holy texts and attending classes or prayer meetings.

2. ATTEND TO YOUR SPIRITUAL GROWTH DAILY

Consider engaging with prayer, meditation, reading inspirational materials and taking stock of your progress on a daily basis. Add any one of these soul-nurturing habits to your routine and when you are comfortable, bring in another one. Be gentle, kind and encouraging to yourself as you work to establish new routines.

Acknowledgments

This book is the product of collaborative effort on many, many levels. I am profoundly grateful to all the women in my lineage. My journey began in your vision and dreams, and has been fueled by your prayers and sacrifices. I am humbled to be standing on your shoulders.

To my mentors and teachers in the healing arts, Mary K Radpour, Michael Penn, William Hatcher, Julie Burns Walker, Jon Connelly, Miela Gruber, Margo Maine, Robert Weinstein, Sarah Gilbert, Ann Marie Garran, Nina Rovinelli Heller, Brenda Kurz, Pete Papallo, and Andy Vengrove: thank you all for walking your noble paths before me and for modeling excellence.

To my sister-friends who have encouraged me through all the ups and downs of writing this book, Vidya, Susan, Beth, Joy, Leigh, Shoreh, Ladan, Ingeborg, Rajaa, Nyaguthii and Faraneh: thank you all for being just one text message away at all times, and for believing that the book could happen.

To the amazing tribe of family and friends that have accompanied me through life at every stage of the journey from organizing wedding make-up to supporting me through loss and everything in-between, you are just too many to name, but you know who you are: thank you all from the bottom of my heart.

My deep gratitude also goes to everyone involved in all stages of the production of this book from idea to finished product and beyond: Lorena Iturrino, Jeff Goins, Kristen Brack, Kim Harper-Kennedy, Caitlin McCrum, Patricia Marshall and Sue Campbell. To my editors Chantel Hamilton and Kirstyn Smith: thank you so much for understanding my vision for this book and for your meticulous care in bringing that vision into being.

To my children Anis and Asiyih: you two teach me so much about nobility. I love you both very dearly and I am extremely honored to be your mom.

To my husband Hamid: thank you for your unwavering support, encouragement and for reading every single draft. It is magic to be walking through life alongside you.

To all my clients: your courage and resilience inspire me each day, and you have all taught me to trust in the power of the human spirit. Thank you!

Notes

Introduction: Welcome!

1. "In the U.S., Decline of Christianity Continues at Rapid Pace: An update on America's changing religious landscape." Pew Research Center, Washington, D.C. (Oct. 17, 2019) https://www.pewforum.org/2019/10/17/in-u-s-decline-of-christianity-continues-at-rapid-pace. Accessed November 1, 2021.

2. Eckhart Tolle, *The Power of Now: A Guide to Spiritual Enlightenment* (Novato, CA: New World Library, 1999), 13.

3. Lisa Miller, Priya Wickramaratne, Marc J. Gameroff et al. (2012). Religiosity And Major Depression In Adults At High Risk: A Ten-Year Prospective Study. *American Journal of Psychiatry* 169 (2012): 89-94, doi.org/10.1176/appi.ajp.2011.10121823.

4. Lisa Miller, *The Awakened Brain: The New Science of Spirituality and our Quest for an Inspired Life* (New York: Random House, 2021), 7.

5. Kenneth Kendler, Charles O Gardener, and Carol A. Prescott. "Religion, psychopathology, and substance use and abuse: A multimeasure, genetic-epidemiologic study," *American Journal of Psychiatry* 154 (1997): 322-29.

6. Michael Inzlicht, Ian McGregor, Jacob B. Hirsh and Kyle Nash, "Neural markers of religious conviction," *Psychological Science* 20, no.3 (2009): 385-92.

7. Lisa Miller, The Spiritual Child: The New Science on Parenting For Health and Lifelong Thriving, accessed June 3, 2021, https://www.lisamillerphd.com/the-spiritual-child.

8. David Lukoff, "Spirituality and Recovery From Serious Mental Problems." In *The Oxford Handbook of Psychology and Spirituality,* ed. Lisa Miller (New York: Oxford University Press, 2012), 419.

9. Jennifer Gaudiani, *Sick Enough: A Guide to the Medical Complications of Eating Disorders* (New York: Routledge, 2019), 32.

10. David DeSteno, *How God Works: The Science Behind the Benefits of Religion* (New York: Simon & Schuster, 2021), 3.

11. Brett Q. Ford, Julia O. Dmitrieva, Daniel Heller et al., "Culture Shapes Whether the Pursuit of Happiness Predicts Higher or Lower Well-Being," *Journal of Experimental Psychology,* 144, no.6 (2015):1053-62, doi.org/10.1037/xge0000108.

12. Soyoung Q. Park, Thorsten Kahnt, Azade Dogan et al., "A neural link between generosity and happiness," *Nature Communications* 8 (2017): 15964 doi.org/10.1038/ncomms15964.

13. Monica M. Matthieu, Karen A. Lawrence, Emma Robertson-Blackmore, "The impact of a civic service program on biopsychosocial outcomes of post 9/11 U.S. military veterans," *Psychiatry Research* 248 (2017): 111-116, doi.org/10.1016/j.psychres.2016.12.028.

14. Louann Brizendine, *The Female Brain* (New York: Three Rivers Press, 2006), xviii-xix.

Chapter 1: Soul, Spirituality and Mental Health

1. Carl G. Jung, *Modern Man in Search of a Soul* (New York: Harcourt, Inc., 1933), 123.

2. Michael Singer, *The Untethered Soul: The Journey Beyond Yourself* (Oakland, CA: New Harbinger Publications, 2007), 28.

3. Lisa Miller, "Introduction," in *The Oxford Handbook of Psychology and Spirituality,* ed. Lisa J. Miller (New York: Oxford University Press, 2012), 2.

4. Merriam-Webster Online Dictionary accessed May 4, 2021, https://www.merriam-webster.com/dictionary/spirit.

5   Merriam-Webster Online Dictionary accessed May 4, 2021, https://www.merriam-webster.com/dictionary/spiritual.

6. Akasha Gloria Hull, *Soul Talk: The New Spirituality of African American Women* (Rochester, VT: Inner Traditions International, 2001), 2.

7. Lisa Miller, *The Spiritual Child: The New Science on Parenting for Health and Lifelong Thriving* (New York: St Martin's Press, 2015), 25.

8. Eileen Eppig, "Worldviews and Women's Spirituality," in *WomanSoul: The Inner Life of Women's Spirituality*, edited by Carole A. Rayburn and Lillian Comas-Diaz (Westport, CT: Preager, 2008), 4.

9. P. Scott Richards, "Honoring Religious Diversity and Universal Spirituality in Psychotherapy," in *The Oxford Handbook of Psychology and Spirituality*, ed. Lisa J. Miller (New York: Oxford University Press, 2012), 244.

10. David DeSteno, *How God Works: The Science Behind the Benefits of Religion* (New York: Simon & Schuster, 2021).

11. P. Scott Richards and Allen E. Bergin, eds. *Handbook of Psychotherapy and Religious Diversity* (Washington, DC: American Psychological Association, 2000).

12. Michael E. Berrett, Randy K. Hardman, and P. Scott Richards, "The Role of Spirituality in Eating Disorder Treatment and Recovery," in *Treatment of Eating Disorders: Bridging the Research-Practice Gap*, eds. Margo Maine, Beth Hartman McGilley and Douglas W. Bunnell (Burlington, MA: Academic Press, 2010), 367.

13. Margo Maine and Douglas W. Bunnell, "A Perfect Biopsychosocial Storm: Gender, Culture, and Eating Disorders" in *Treatment of Eating Disorders: Bridging the Research-Practice Gap*, eds. Margo Maine, Beth Hartman McGilley and Douglas W. Bunnell (Burlington, MA: Academic Press, 2010), 8.

Chapter 2: What Does It Mean to Be a Woman?

1. bell hooks, *The Will to Change: Men, Masculinity, and Love* (New York: Washington Square Press, 2004), 18.

2. Gerda Lerner, *The Creation of Patriarchy* (New York: Oxford University Press, 1986), 239.

3. Allan G. Johnson, *The Gender Knot: Unravelling Our Patriarchal Legacy* (Philadelphia, PA: Temple University Press, 2014), 37.

4. John Bradshaw, *Creating Love: The Next Great Stage of Growth* (New York: Bantam Books), 26.

5. Christine Kuehner, "Why is Depression More Common Among Women than Among Men?" *Lancet Psychiatry* 4, no.2 (2017 Feb.): 146-158.

6. Carmen P. McLean, Anu Asnaani, Brett T. Litz and Stefan G. Hoffman, "Gender Differences in Anxiety Disorders: Prevalence, Course of Illness, Comorbidity and Burden of Illness," *J Psychiatry Res.* 45, no. 8 (2011 August): 1027-1035. doi.org/10.1016/j.jpsychires.2011.03.006.

7. N. Breslau, H. D. Chilcoat, R. C. Kessler, E. L. Peterson and V. C. Lucia, "Vulnerability to assaultive violence: further specification of the sex difference in post-traumatic stress disorder," *Psychol Med.* 29, no. 4(1999): 813-21. doi.org/10.1017/s0033291799008612.

8. Margo Maine and Douglas W. Bunnell, "A Perfect Biopsychosocial Storm: Gender, Culture, and Eating Disorders" in *Treatment of Eating Disorders: Bridging the Research-Practice Gap*, eds. Margo Maine, Beth Hartman McGilley and Douglas W. Bunnell (Burlington, MA: Academic Press, 2010), 3.

9. "Gender and Women's Health," World Health Organization, accessed January 5, 2021, https://www.who.int/mental_health/prevention/genderwomen/en/.

10. Maureen Murdock, *The Heroine's Journey: A Woman's Quest for Wholeness* (Boulder, CO: Shambhala Publications, Inc., 2020), 57.

11. Louann Brizindine, *The Female Brain* (New York: Three Rivers Press, 2006), 8.

12. Maureen Murdock, *The Heroine's Journey: A Woman's Quest for Wholeness* (Boulder, CO: Shambhala Publications, Inc., 2020), 16.

13. Augusto Lopez-Claros and Bahiyyih Nakhjavani, *Equality for Women = Prosperity for All: The Disastrous Global Crisis of Gender Inequality* (New York: St. Martin's Press, 2018).

14. Joshua Miller and Ann Marie Garran, *Racism in the United States: Implications for Helping Professionals* (Belmont, CA: Brooks/Cole, 2008), 4.

15. Joshua Miller and Ann Marie Garran, *Racism in the United States: Implications for Helping Professionals* (Belmont, CA: Brooks/Cole, 2008), 135.

16. Isabel Wilkerson, *Caste: The Origins of Our Discontents* (New York: Random House, 2020), 387.

17. Kathie Carlson, *In Her Image* (Boulder, CO: Shambhala Publications, Inc., 1990), 77.

18. Louann Brizindine, *The Female Brain* (New York: Three Rivers Press, 2006), 8.

19. Louann Brizindine, *The Female Brain* (New York: Three Rivers Press, 2006), 13.

20. Tarana Burke, *Unbound: My Story of Liberation and the Birth of the Me Too Movement* (New York: Flatiron Books, 2021).

21. Polly Young-Eisendrath and Florence Wiedemann, *Female Authority: Empowering Women Through Psychotherapy* (New York: Guilford Press, 1987), 119.

22. Maya Angelou, *Phenomenal Woman: Four Poems Celebrating Women* (New York: Random House, 1994), 3.

Chapter 3: Mine Your Inner Gems

1. Carl G. Jung, *Modern Man in Search of a Soul* (New York: Harcourt, Inc., 1933).

2. Sarah Y. Krakauer, *Treating Dissociative Identity Disorder: The Power of the Collective Heart* (New York: Routledge, 2001), 44.

3. Jon Connelly, *Life Changing Conversations with Rapid Resolution Therapy: A Single Conversation Can be a Life-Changing Event* (Jon Connelly, 2019), 117.

4. Linda Kavelin Popov, *Sacred Moments: Daily Meditations on the Virtues* (Hixson, TN: Images International, 2003), 1.

5. Richard Schwartz, *No Bad Parts: Healing Trauma and Restoring Wholeness with the Internal Family Systems Model* (Boulder, CO: Sounds True, 2021), 1.

6. The Virtues Project, accessed January 20, 2022, https://thevirtuesproject.com

7. Diane Morgan, *Essential Islam: A Comprehensive Guide to Belief and Practice* (Santa Barbara, CA: Praeger, 2010).

8. Dovie Schochet "What are the 13 Attributes of Mercy?" accessed 8 October 2021, https://www.chabad.org/parshah/article_cod/aid/3609722/jewish/What-Are-the-13-attributes.

9: Matthew 5:3-10

10. 2 Peter 1:5-7

11. Genesis 1:26

12. Deborah Christensen and Julie Burns Walker, *From Self-Awareness to Transformation: Reflecting on the Journey to the True Self with Tools to Assist the Process* (Wilmette, IL: Oneness Model Series, 2007), 18.

Recollections: The Lion and the Deer

1. Alana Fairchild, *Rumi Oracle: An Invitation into the Heart of the Divine* (Glen Waverley, Victoria: Blue Angel Publishing, 2021), 102.

2. Alana Fairchild, *Rumi Oracle: An Invitation into the Heart of the Divine* (Glen Waverley, Victoria: Blue Angel Publishing, 2021), 103.

Chapter 4: Embrace Your Duality

1. "Two Wolves: A Cherokee Legend," accessed on April 17, 2021, https://www.firstpeople.us/FP-Html-Legends/TwoWolves-Cherokee.html.

2. Marianne Williamson, *A Return to Love: Reflections on the Principles of A COURSE IN MIRACLES* (New York: HarperOne, 2012), 190.

3. Jennifer Gaudiani, *Sick Enough: A Guide to the Medical Complications of Eating Disorders* (New York: Routledge, 2019), 101.

4. Sigmund Freud, *The Ego and the Id* (New York: W.W. Norton & Company, 1990).

5. Ed Halliwell, "How Taming the Mind is like Riding a Horse," Mindful-Healthy Mind, Healthy Life, May 4, 2016, accessed on 9 December, 2021, https://www.mindful.org/how-taming-the-mind-is-like-riding-a-horse.

Chapter 5: Know Your Purpose

1. Oxford Languages accessed June 19, 2021, https://www.google.com/search?q=purpose+dictionary.

2. Brené Brown, *The Gifts of Imperfection: Let Go of Who You Think You're Supposed to Be and Embrace Who You Are - Your Guide to a Wholehearted Life* (Center City, MN: Hazelden, 2010), 112.

3. Adapted from the Ruhi Institute, *Teaching Children's Classes Grade 1, Book 3.* (West Palm Beach, Florida: Palabra Publications, 1995), 10.

Chapter 6: Build Authentic Relationships

1. William S. Hatcher, Love, Power and Justice: The Dynamics of Authentic Morality (Wilmette, IL: Bahá'í Publishing Trust, 2002), 5.

2. Mary K. Radpour in collaboration with The Authenticity Project, *Inner Freedom & Self-Mastery: The Dynamics of Moral Authenticity* (Hixon, TN: Images International, 2002), 14.

3. Mary K. Radpour in collaboration with The Authenticity Project, *Inner Freedom & Self-Mastery: The Dynamics of Moral Authenticity* (Hixon, TN: Images International, 2002), 14.

4. Jonathan Haidt, *The Righteous Mind: Why Good People are Divided by Politics and Religion* (New York: Vintage Books, 2013), 80.

5. Ijeoma Oluo, *So You Want to Talk About Race* (New York: Seal Press, 2019), 27.

6. Isabel Wilkerson, *Caste: The Origins of Our Discontents* (New York: Random House, 2020), 64.

7. Isabel Wilkerson, *Caste: The Origins of Our Discontents* (New York: Random House, 2020), 66.

8. Richard Rothstein, *The Color of Law: A Forgotten History of How Our Government Segregated America* (New York: Liveright, 2017).

9. "Multiracial in America—Chapter 5: Race and Social Connections—Friends, Family and Neighborhoods." Pew Research Center, Washington, D.C. (June 11, 2015) https://www.pewresearch.org/social- trends/2015/06/11/chapter-5-race-and-social-connections- friends-family-and-neighborhoods. Accessed November 7, 2021.

10. William S. Hatcher, Love, Power and Justice: The Dynamics of Authentic Morality (Wilmette, IL: Bahá'í Publishing Trust, 2002), 28.

Chapter 7: Lean into Hardship

1. Marianne Williamson, *Romantic Relationships: Talks on Spirituality and Modern Life* (New York: Hay House, 2004).

2. Luvvie Ajayi Jones, *Professional Trouble Maker: The Fear-Fighter Manual* (New York: Viking, 2021).

3. Jon Connelly, *Life Changing Conversations with Rapid Resolution Therapy: A Single Conversation Can be a Life-Changing Event* (Jon Connelly, 2019), 7.

4. Lawrence G. Calhoun and Richard G. Tedeschi, eds. *Handbook of Posttraumatic Growth: Research and Practice.* (New York: Routledge, 2006).

5. Pema Chödrön, *The Wisdom of No Escape and The Path of Loving-Kindness* (Boulder, CO: Shambhala Publications, 1991), 34.

6. Eckhart Tolle, *The Power of Now: A Guide to Spiritual Enlightenment (*Novato, CA: New World Library, 1999), 38.

7. Khalil Gibran, *The Prophet,* (SDE Classics, 2019), 27.

8. Jalaluddin Rumi, "Childhood Friends," in *The Essential Rumi,* by Coleman Barks (San Francisco, CA: Harper, 1995).

9. Glennon Doyle, *Untamed* (New York: The Dial Press, 2020), 77.

Chapter 8: Develop a Spiritual Practice

1. Stephen Schwartz and Larry Dossey, "Nonlocality, Intention, and Observer Effects in Healing Studies: Laying a Foundation for the Future." In *The Oxford Handbook of Psychology and Spirituality*, ed. Lisa J. Miller (New York: Oxford University Press, 2012), 544.

2. Richard J. Davidson, Jon Kabat-Zinn, Jessica Schumacher et al., "Alterations in brain and immune function produced by mindfulness meditation," *Psychosom Med.* 65, no. 4 (2003): 564-70, doi.org/10.1097/01.psy.0000077505.67574.e3

3. Britta K. Hölzel, James Carmody, Mark Vangel et al., "Mindfulness Practice Leads to Increases in Regional Brain

165

Gray Matter," *Psychiatry Res.* 191, no. 1 (Jan 30, 2011): 36-43, doi.org/10.1016/j.pscychresns.2010.08.006.

4. Elizabeth A. Hoge, Eric Bui, Sophie A. Palitz, et al., "The Effect of Mindfulness Meditation Training on Biological Acute Stress Responses in Generalized Anxiety Disorder." *Psychiatry Res.* 262 (2018):328-332, doi.org/10.1016/j.psychres.2017.01.006.

5. Eben Alexander, *Proof of Heaven: A Neurosurgeon's Journey into the Afterlife* (New York: Simon & Schuster, 2012), 130.

6. Brené Brown, *The Gifts of Imperfection: Let Go of Who You Think You're Supposed to Be and Embrace Who You Are - Your Guide to a Wholehearted Life* (Center City, MN: Hazelden, 2010), 4.

About the Author

KADZO KANGWANA is a licensed clinical social worker specializing in the treatment of trauma and eating disorders. When she is not working with clients, she facilitates workshops on spiritual development. Kadzo has an MA in clinical mental health counseling from Union University and an MSW from the University of Connecticut. Kadzo's first career was in wildlife conservation, and she holds a BA in zoology from the University of Oxford and a PhD from the University of Cambridge. Kadzo's life has spanned four continents, and her broad experience informs her work with clients of all backgrounds.

Receive a free workbook when you subscribe to Kadzo's email list at kadzokangwana.com.